# EPIPHANY

# MICHAEL COREN

## EPIPHANY

### A CHRISTIAN'S CHANGE OF HEART & MIND OVER SAME-SEX MARRIAGE

SIGNAL
McCLELLAND
& STEWART

Library and Archives Canada Cataloguing in Publication
information available on request

ISBN: 978-0-7710-2411-5
eBook ISBN: 978-0-7710-2412-2

Published simultaneously in the United States of America
by McClelland & Stewart, a division of Penguin Random House Canada Limited

Library of Congress Control Number is available upon request.

Printed and bound in the United States of America

McClelland & Stewart,
a division of Penguin Random House Canada Limited,
a Penguin Random House Company

www.penguinrandomhouse.ca

1 2 3 4 5  20 19 18 17 16

*To my daughter Lucy. So wise.*

# CONTENTS

*Acknowledgements*

ix

*Introduction*

1

SO THIS IS HOW IT FEELS

9

BIBLE BELIEVING

49

ON THE FRONT LINE

111

THE FUTURE

147

LAST WORDS

195

*Notes*

217

# ACKNOWLEDGEMENTS

A book is always far more than its words and in this case particularly so. In the past three years, I have met with and spoken to so many people in the gay community, to gay Christians, and to liberal Christians that I could never name them all. I have also spoken to many people who are dramatically opposed to gay equality and to a more progressive understanding of Christianity and I am sure they would rather they were not named. That's fine with me. I am and will continue to be immensely grateful to those men and women who gave me their time and knowledge, especially when they weren't entirely sure of my intentions. Because there are so many people whom I should thank and acknowledge, any list will be by its nature severely inadequate and even disappointing. Please forgive me. My thanks are not just for those who spoke to me about the actual subject of this book but also for those whose own life and experience bled its way into my life and my soul. Some of these people are gay, some are not; some are Christian, some are not; some are gay and Christian, some are not; some are journalists, priests, activists, and academics or a combination of the three, some are not. What unites them is that they enabled me to write this book, a work of which I am extremely proud. My thanks to Reverend Brent Hawkes, Travis Myers, Emma Teitel, Reverend Tom Decker, Michael McKenzie, John Mraz, Shaun Proulx, Andrea Houston, Reverend Professor Diarmaid MacCulloch, Bishop Alan Wilson,

Fr. Pearce Carefoot, Canon Susan Bell, Dean Douglas Stoute, John Moore, Reverend Bruce Myers, Don Beyers, Archbishop Colin Johnson, Maurice Tomlinson, Stephen Hayhurst, Adam Goldenberg, Mary Conliffe, Robert Turner, Grant Jahnke; to Jonathan Kay at *The Walrus* and Andrew Phillips at the *Toronto Star* for publishing my writing on this issue and thus bringing so many new people to my attention; and to Douglas Pepper and those at Signal McClelland & Stewart and Penguin Random House who agreed to take the chance to publish a very different book by a very different Michael Coren.

# EPIPHANY

# INTRODUCTION

THIS BOOK IS NOT IN any way supposed to be the last word, certainly not the first word or even the best word about such a profound, important, and public as well as personal and emotional issue as equal marriage. But it is certainly my word, and as such I stand by it totally and proudly. It is the account of how a heterosexual, married man, a Christian author and broadcaster who was well known for opposing same-sex marriage and was in Canada arguably the institution's most high-profile opponent, came to be not only a passionate defender of marriage equality but also a champion of gay rights and an outspoken campaigner for full acceptance of gay people into the Christian church. Because of that fact, the first chapter of the book is my personal story of what happened, how I came to change my mind and my opinions, and what I experienced – positive as well as negative – when I did so. It's a story not only of a change of view and politics but of a change of life and belief. It's also an intensely Christian story, and that is something I wish to emphasize. I changed on this issue not in spite of being a Christian but precisely because I *am* a Christian, and my faith has deepened and broadened as I have come to appreciate the need for a new understanding of same-sex love and gays' relationships within the Christian church and the Christian world.

The rest of the book is diverse and rather different from other works on the issue. It presents the Christian arguments for gay equality and equal marriage and thus looks at the traditional and well-versed reasons for the opposing point of view; it devotes an entire chapter to recounting the testimonies of people who are Christian and gay. I also speculate on the future of the Christian response to equal marriage. Not all of it is new territory, of course, and I am certainly not the first person to re-address the alleged Biblical opposition to homosexuality or discuss what may be evidence of scriptural tolerance of same-sex relationships but I hope I can bring a fresh perspective to all of this and, if not, can stand on the shoulders of those who have gone before me. Without any risk of hyperbole, I can say that the issue of homosexuality is one of the most – perhaps the most – significant and pressing challenges facing contemporary Christianity. Unless and until we can establish a new understanding of same-sex attraction and of gay people, we cannot and will not be listened to by the new generation of people living in the Western world, who simply cannot comprehend opposition to the aspirations and relationships of their gay friends and neighbours. And I don't blame them for reacting in such a way and congratulate them for their empathy and compassion. Relevance and appeal cannot and must not, naturally, dictate theology or shape truth, and if I thought that scripture and Christianity opposed full gay membership of the church and marriage equality, I would say and write so, whatever the consequences. But I do not. It is my sincere belief that there is absolutely no need to compromise Christian orthodoxy or absolute truth as we construct a new Christian conversation and understanding about homosexuality and I hope I can convince others of that reality.

This book is not in itself a sociological, political, or secular argument for marriage equality. Frankly, those debates have already taken place and for the most part in the Western world have been won. When I do touch on sociology, politics, and general questions of sexuality and social discussion, they will be in passing and be used to qualify or explain the greater theological point. Christian opponents of equal marriage tend to mingle secular homophobia with what they regard as moral and religious objections when they make their arguments. There is an abundance of general material out there concerning homosexuality and same-sex marriage in its various contexts but, again, this book is specifically Christian, albeit written for all people whatever their faith or lack of one. The church is part of society, those within the church function in society, and the relationship between church and society is a vital one. I realize that some people, especially those hurt by Christians, would prefer it were not so but the church will continue – thank God – and I feel I owe it to my faith and to gay Christians who wish to be accepted and to secular gay people who are still so hurt by Christian hostility, to try to put matters right. This book is not a Christian excuse but a Christian explanation, a plea for a revolutionary understanding of Christ's love and God's grace.

There are also those in the gay community who might argue that the campaign for equal marriage is irrelevant to them and even a digression from their genuine struggle. Some might believe that marriage itself is an aspect of a patriarchal society, has long enforced male dominance over women, and perhaps led to greater hatred of gays. Thus, they would argue, the institution of marriage has absolutely nothing to do with gay rights. It's an argument that some, in particular in the lesbian feminist movement, espouse, and while I understand their argument I know of too many gay women as well as men who reject it. I myself do the same because I believe in the religious, moral, and social importance of stable, lasting, committed, and recognized unions. Nobody is forced to marry but nobody should be forced not to do so.

I will inevitably sometimes use words that do not pass the ever-changing litmus test of politically correct language and, if we are honest about it, sometimes the list of the included and, thus, the excluded becomes laborious. I understand that the term *queer* has been liberated from the abusive and is now used in a generic manner but I do not use it in this book. I was born in 1959 and the word was used to denigrate and abuse. As a straight man, I just don't feel comfortable with it.

I am also aware that LGBT, LBTQ, LGBTQ, or LGBTQI (lesbian, gay, bisexual, transgender, queer or questioning, and intersex ) is often preferred but I have simply used the term *gay* – partly because it is simpler and, to me at least, more acceptable and gentle and also because I have neither the scope, expertise, nor mandate to write about issues concerning trans people in this relatively brief volume. Please forgive my errors and know I mean no disrespect. I realize that, for example, transgendered or bisexual people sometimes feel excluded by various terms that are used by gay as well as straight people, and while I will and do try my best not to offend, it is possible at times I will. This is never my intention. I am, as are all of us, a work in process and progress.

Also, I am not an authority on gay history, gay politics, or the gay community and would never have the audacity to claim otherwise. I make no apology for that and hope and believe that it gives this book a certain advantage: it is supposed to be a general and broad argument based on the experiences and learning of one straight man and his yet-to-be-completed journey. I am, I suppose, trying to convert as well as support, and preaching to the choir is generally a waste of time. Some of what I write will also no doubt upset some gay people because this is mostly a specifically Christian response to complex issues of sexuality and relationships, and while I have fully accepted the potential beauty of committed same-sex partnerships, I retain a Christ-centred respect for faithful and committed marriage between two people. I appreciate that this is not the view of all of those who will read this book, gay and straight, but I have come to learn more than ever that respectful disagreement is a fundamental weapon against fundamentalist intolerance.

There are those who might argue that this is not my struggle, that I have no vested or personal interest or, as one person put it rather clumsily, that I have no skin in the game. I suppose it would be like telling a Gentile that they should not oppose anti-Semitism or a white person that they had no business opposing racism. My interest as a Christian, and particularly one who got things so wrong for so long, is truth, love, compassion, and justice. As for the latter, there is also a vested interest in that, as I said earlier and will repeat later, unless the church can find its way to a new, loving, and accepting relationship with gay people, it will be considered at best irrelevant and at worst downright bigoted by the new and next generation. It would be tragic if that were allowed to happen.

To a certain degree, this book is about what I believe the Christian attitude should be toward gay people rather than gay marriage in that if we accept same-sex attraction, we will as a direct and inevitable consequence accept same-sex marriage as well. There are, of course, differences and nuances and there are certainly people both within and outside of the church who are open to homosexuality but refuse to embrace full marriage equality. I don't quite understand that approach because equality surely has to be complete and total if it is to be an equality worth the name. Also, in Christian terms, because of the importance of marriage, it would be visibly discriminatory to embrace an openly gay presence in the Christian community but insist that those people who are apparently so welcome are not welcome to enter the institution that Christians hold so dear. But, as I say, many of the arguments I make and experiences I record could be applied to the general welcoming of gay people as well as to an active support for marriage equality.

At the end of June 2015, the Supreme Court of the United States made marriage equality legal throughout the country. The ruling was complex, thorough, and at times lyrical, epitomized by its conclusion: "No union is more profound than marriage, for it embodies the highest ideals of love, fidelity, devotion, sacrifice, and family. In forming a marital union, two people become something greater than once they were. As some of the petitioners in these cases demonstrate, marriage embodies a love that may endure even past death. It would misunderstand these men and women to say they disrespect the idea of marriage. Their plea is that they do respect it, respect it so deeply that they seek to find its fulfillment for themselves. Their hope is not to be condemned to live in loneliness, excluded from one of civilization's oldest institutions. They ask for equal dignity in the eyes of the law. The Constitution grants them that right. The judgment of the Court of Appeals for the Sixth Circuit is reversed."

Much indeed needs to be reversed. This is the story of a pilgrimage and, yes, a reversal if you like. It is also a gesture of apology and contrition. I have got and done things wrong over the years and caused harm and pain. I am most deeply sorry. I am also very optimistic. The late Father Jim Cotter was an Anglican priest who bravely championed gay marriage and rights in the earliest stages of the church equality movement. He wrote twenty-five years ago: "There are four stages in the church's response to any challenge to its tradition. First, it pretends the challenge isn't there. Secondly it opposes it vehemently. Thirdly, it starts to admit extenuations and exceptions. Finally it says: 'That's what we really thought all along'." The former Bishop of California, William Swing, a relatively conservative Episcopalian, put it another way when asked by journalists how he spoke to his Christian flock about the devastating effect of AIDS and HIV on the gay community in the 1980s. "Sometimes I want to say to them that God became man, why don't you try it?" Quite so. Where love is, God is. Where humanity is, understanding is. And now it begins.

# SO THIS IS HOW IT FEELS

I AM NOT GAY, NEVER have been, and doubt very much I ever will be. I am a Christian who is a member of the Anglican Communion, more specifically a member of the Anglican Church of Canada and more specifically still an Anglo-Catholic Christian who until the end of 2013 was an intensely observant and serious Roman Catholic and, I suppose, one of the most high-profile Roman Catholic media figures and Catholic apologists in Canada and also relatively well-known as a Roman Catholic journalist, author, and speaker in the United States, Britain, and elsewhere. I wrote two best-selling books about Catholicism and one of them, *Why Catholics Are Right*, was on the best-seller list for ten weeks, was translated into several languages, and sold extensively. I was a biweekly columnist for *The Catholic Register*, Canada's national Catholic weekly newspaper, and a monthly columnist for the *Catholic World Report* in the United States, *Catholic Insight*, and the self-identified "pro-family" newspaper *The Interim* in North America. I was also a frequent contributor to Britain's *Catholic Herald* and to various international Catholic and socially conservative publications and was frequently called upon to speak for Catholic and socially conservative causes on television and radio. I was one of the busiest speakers on the Catholic lecture circuit in Canada and the United States, won numerous awards, received a papal knighthood for my services to Catholic media, was made Columnist of the Year for all of North America in the Catholic

Press Awards in 2013, and won numerous other Catholic media prizes; in 2011 I was also given the Archbishop Adam Exner Award for Catholic Excellence in Public Life in Canada. I was a regular guest on the Catholic television network EWTN, the syndicated radio show *Catholic Answers*, and several other Catholic radio shows internationally. I was also about to be given my own Catholic radio talk show in the United States. No less than New York's Cardinal Timothy Dolan told a media scrum that my article on Pope Francis was one of the best analyses that he'd read![1]

Outside of specifically Catholic media, I was a weekly columnist for the conservative Sun newspaper chain in Canada with an enormous readership in daily newspapers in Toronto, Calgary, Edmonton, Ottawa, and Winnipeg; for thirteen years I hosted a nightly current affairs show on CTS, a Christian-based television station, and for four years hosted a nightly program on Sun News, the Canadian version of Fox News in the United States. I won several awards for the former show. I was also an award-winning host for one of the largest talk radio stations in Canada.

And in all of these places I argued – when the subject arose – against same-sex marriage, presented the orthodox and even conservative Catholic or Christian case for opposing marriage equality, and spoke out against many of the aspirations of the gay community. I was even the recipient of the RTNDA Award, a major media prize, for co-hosting a public debate that was broadcast on national radio on same-sex marriage where I spoke, of course, against the motion. I was somewhat of a darling of the Christian right, a bloody hero for many social conservatives who believed themselves without a voice. So what went so terribly wrong?

Let me emphasize that in spite of what some people may have thought and said I never hated and never deliberately infected any of my opinions with malice or dislike. I don't write this as an excuse or a justification and nor am I worried about being condemned – I have experienced so much of that in the past two years from my former allies that I have become immune – but because it simply is true. I never hated because I couldn't. I had too many gay friends, had been helped by too many gay people, and just did not care viscerally or emotionally about the issue. But in a way this makes my behaviour worse because I knew better. It's not that I was dishonest or disingenuous but that more than anything I was dogmatic. Once I'd taken up the banner of anti–marriage equality, it became increasingly difficult to cast it off. I suppose I may sound weak or even pathetic and cowardly but it's nevertheless the truth.

I grew up in an intensely secular home on the edge of London, England. Three of my grandparents were Jewish, but my mother's mother – and it's the maternal line that has to be Jewish – was not. My parents weren't only secular but as Jews or "sort of" Jews they had known even in generally tolerant or indifferent Britain what discrimination was like. This was the 1960s and 70s, and homosexuality was mentioned only in whispers. When people like my parents used the word *queer* – which was pretty much the only word used for gay people – it was from them less pejorative than descriptive. The only acceptable face of homosexuality was on television, with comics camping it up and playing effeminate stereotypes all the while assuring their public that in real life they could barely keep their pants on when an attractive woman walked past. They were, of course, all gay men off camera but never the caricatures they created on TV. If they'd revealed their secret, their careers would probably have been over. From a working-class home, I was propelled into university and then into London literary society, where I first encountered, at least in its inchoate stages, a proud and openly gay community. My first book, released in 1984,[2] came about with the help of a highly respected and extremely gay theatre critic named Jim Hiley, who had very kindly recommended me to a publisher. There was no other way a twenty-five-year-old would have landed a book contract. Then I went to work at the *New Statesman*, the country's premier left-leaning magazine, when the late and great Christopher Hitchens still was on the staff. Ours was a masthead full of privately educated, clever, good-looking boys all seduced by socialism and many of them ambivalent about their sexuality or openly gay. Homosexual influence was everywhere we looked, but still outside of specific areas none of us dared speak its name, or at least said it just a little too quietly.

In 1985 after almost a year of instruction from a delightful if bitingly conservative priest, I joined the Roman Catholic Church, which then led and still in many ways leads the culture war against gay rights but employs more gay men than any other institution in the world. If that claim appears to be exaggerated, hysterical, or malicious, I assure you that it is none of those things. Many of these men are celibate, but numerous gay priests are in relationships, which makes the whole thing even more absurd. In a later chapter of this book, I interview gay Christians and I have included three gay men who were formerly ordained Roman Catholic clergy. Believe me, I could fill the entire book with such interviews. The Roman Catholic Church is certainly not full of hatred and homophobia but it has, as with some elements of the Protestant right, elevated the issue to a level that has no basis in scripture. As I explain in some length later, Jesus never mentions same-sex attraction, lesbianism is not referred to at all in the Old Testament, the letters of the Apostles mention homosexuality only briefly, and what references to homosexuality that do exist make up a tiny, insignificant sliver of theological texts, a splash of minutiae within the primary Christian text and the basis of the Christian faith. But the gay issue has become the prism through which myriad conservative Christians judge not only their but other people's faith, morality, and conviction. It's tragic, reductive, and destructive on so many levels but, again, more of that later. As a newly minted Catholic in Britain and then, after I married a Canadian and came to live in Canada in 1987 as a loyal Catholic journalist, I was thrown into the marriage debate and I wrote and broadcast about the issue many times, defending the doctrine I had adopted as part of my converted creed. The issue was never a major part of my work but, goodness me, it sometimes felt like it. And I'm sure to gays and lesbians, who were understandably more interested in my views on them than my opinions on the Middle East, taxation policies, or international trade, for example, I probably became something of a monster. I said some very careless things and at the very least empowered those who genuinely did have a hateful agenda.

I tried to be compassionate and empathetic in my arguments but didn't try hard enough and because of that – and I don't blame them – some of the more extreme gay activists insulted and abused me and even tried to have me fired. On one occasion, a leading political figure in Toronto approached the publisher of a newspaper for which I wrote a column and insisted that I be let go. My employer didn't necessarily agree with me but he believed that my right to speak my mind was sacrosanct. On another occasion, a gay activist contacted various companies and businesses and asked them to withdraw their advertising until and unless a television network on which I hosted a daily show terminated my contract. The various businesses did not respond and the network defended me. I was, over the years, subjected to many obscene and angry tweets, e-mails and letters, and threats. Not, however, anywhere near as many as I was to experience later on when I changed my thinking about all of this and had to contend with the unleashed anger of the Christian right. It was like watching a clash of ideas through the other side of the window, and what I saw revolted me and made me feel deeply ashamed.

The change, the conversion on the road to the rainbow, was incremental and multi-faceted and I don't suppose I will ever be able to properly articulate all of the reasons, the processes, and the stages. The first I realized that there was a problem was when my Christian life, my devotional life, my prayer life, kept running into obstacles, to dead ends, and to painful realizations that the quintessence of the Christ I so worshipped was and is love and that in my stance and statements concerning homosexuality I was not living that love. I realize that to non-Christians, that might sound obscure, irrelevant, or even absurd but none of this makes any sense unless you see me as someone struggling to be a follower of Christ. On a personal level, I felt as if I was being torn and battered. Honesty has to be a central plank of this book, and I say now what I have never publicly revealed before: there were times when I wept at the thought that God was disappointed in me and that much of what I had said and written had caused harm rather than good and had divided rather than united. It caused enormous inner pain.

Anybody who had read my writing, watched me on television, and read between the lines may have realized what was happening, but by the middle of 2013 it was becoming obvious, at least to me. In August all of this was brought into sharp focus by, paradoxically, the Ugandan government. Yes, God bless the lunatic homophobes of Ugandan politics because they changed my life. Those people in that nation who happen to have such a biting obsession with the gay community and such a chronic and violent homophobia brought me to my senses. Canada's then foreign minister, John Baird, had gently and entirely correctly criticized a Kampala official about proposed legislation to further criminalize homosexuality, even going so far as to make it a capital offence. Baird, a Conservative Party stalwart who was no friend of liberals, had long been a great defender of persecuted Christians and was merely speaking up for another persecuted minority group. But instead of being thanked, he was immediately and stridently condemned by those very conservative Christian groups who had previously praised him for his work. How dare he, they shouted, criticize noble Uganda and question the country's political autonomy and independence. Suddenly all these far-right social conservatives were pretending they opposed Western chauvinism and colonial attitudes toward Africa – it would have been laughable if it weren't so repugnant. I was outraged at Uganda's homophobia and outraged at the treatment of Baird, and I said so on television, on radio, and in print. I invited the leader of one of these conservative Christian groups to come on to my television show and explain her anger, which she did. I asked her how she could not be revolted by the idea that people could be executed for being homosexual. She said the policy was "unwise." I was incredulous but not rude and insisted that she was being unfair to the government minister in question and severely unfeeling toward Ugandans with same-sex attraction. This was not only murderous and barbaric, I argued, but was also anti-Christian.

The interview was watched by a few thousand people on television but by many more on the Internet as various social conservatives posted it on their sites as proof that I was becoming horribly soft and selling out. Here was the evidence that their suspicions were justified. Coren had become a friend of the gays! I was swamped with nasty messages and abuse and all for saying what were surely the most self-evident things: it's wrong to kill people because of their sexuality and Jesus wasn't a fan of mass slaughter. At this point, remember, I hadn't said that I supported equal marriage and hadn't really said very much at all other than that people should not be persecuted because of their sexuality. But I began to realize just how raw and how over-sensitive and angry myriad opponents of the gay community genuinely were, and I understood that the opposition to marriage equality was frequently motivated not by a sense of duty to defend traditional wedlock but by a profound dislike of gays and lesbians. Of course, not every critic of marriage equality is like this but, goodness me, those who were expressed themselves loudly and in large numbers and my experience since then has not led me to change my estimation.

In March 2014, I broadcast a commentary on my television show about World Vision, the largest evangelical Christian charity in the world, with around 45,000 employees and annual revenues of more than $2 billion. It does wonderful work feeding and curing the poor and needy in the developing world and usually keeps arms-length from anything controversial. Not now. I said this:

"Last week the aid organization World Vision announced that it would employ Christians living in same-sex marriages. This, we have to realize, was a massive announcement. There seemed to be no pressure for World Vision to change its previously strict code of sexual ethics that declared that no employees could indulge in sex outside of marriage and that marriage was between one man and one woman but still they did so because, we assume, some people at World Vision obviously realized that there were Christians who wanted to help the poor and starving and broken and sick who happened to be gay and had made life-long commitments to their same-sex partners. Within moments of the announcement, however, the evangelical and wider Christian world went into retaliatory over-drive. Leading pastor and author Rick Warren, Billy Graham's son Franklin, and the leaders of entire denominations suggested that donation money would disappear unless World Vision changed their minds and some even advised their congregants to withhold financial support. It was a virtual boycott. World Vision's behaviour was, they claimed, totally unacceptable and there was talk of the evil one, of dark forces, and of hell. Then, lo and behold, it was announced by World Vision that they had reversed their position, that they were very sorry, and that it wouldn't happen again. In less than two days, they had fundamentally and theologically changed their beliefs over a point of profound moral understanding and ethical teaching. Frankly, it's all been a hugely messy, humiliating, and embarrassing affair, and all sorts of people should be ashamed of themselves. Yet many of those people seem proud rather than sorry. What I can't understand is what the marital status or sexuality of someone has to do with their heartfelt desire to help starving African children or Indian families living on the street. Can gay people in committed, lifelong relationships not clean wounds, not hold the dying, not empathize with the desperate? Perhaps, it could be argued, they can do so more successfully than someone who has not been marginalized by mainstream society and by certain churches. Can a gay person in a committed, lifelong partnership not raise money for the starving and work tirelessly for the poorest of the poor? It seems to me they have been doing so for decades and generations and have often done it rather well but we simply have not known about their sexuality. Because, you see, it doesn't matter. Lastly, and most importantly, can gay people actually form committed, lifelong partnerships? Well, obviously not as well as the millions of heterosexuals who have embraced divorce, sometimes serial divorce, and have reduced and decayed the institution of marriage to a sham and a shame. For an organization with the word 'vision' in its name, your blindness is difficult to understand or forgive."

So, there it was. That commentary generated a second wave of hateful letters and complaints as well as some cancelled speaking engagements. The real outpouring was still to come. I was being forced to make a decision and to rethink where I stood and what I believed and said. It was a difficult but invigorating time, like a new conversion, and I felt that I had to take a stand at this point and at least partially introduce my new self to the world. In June 2014, I devoted my weekly column in the Sun newspaper chain to the subject. At the risk of sounding rhetorical, it rather changed my life. Forgive me quoting it in full but here it is:

"I haven't been asked to lead any marches at Pride this year and, frankly, I doubt that's ever likely to happen! I'm still regarded by many in the gay community as an enemy and I understand that reaction. I have said and written things in the past that, while never intentionally hateful, caused offence and pain. This isn't necessarily relevant, in that truth cannot change according to response, but I could and would not say such things any longer. I was wrong. In the past six months I have been parachuted into clouds of new realization and empathy regarding gay issues, largely and ironically because of the angry and hateful responses of some people to my defence of persecuted gay men and women in Africa and Russia. I saw an aspect of the anti-gay movement that shocked me. This wasn't reasonable opposition but a tainted monomania with no understanding of humanity and an obsession with sex rather than love.

"I'm used to threats and abuse, and as someone who has just completed a book about Islam's treatment of Christians and has campaigned for years for beleaguered Christians in the Muslim world I am immune to verbal attacks and even death threats. But this was different. I was accused of betraying my faith. Thing is, I have evolved my position on this issue not in spite of but precisely because of my Catholicism. My belief in God, Christ, the Eucharist, and Christian moral teaching are stronger than ever. Goodness, I am even trying to forgive those 'Christians' who are trying to have my speeches cancelled and have devoted pages on their websites and blogs to my apparent disgrace.

"The other attack is to argue that I have surrendered to pressure or that my children have influenced me. This is so absurd to be genuinely funny. My kids? They're not political, respect and love me and would, anyway, never waste their time trying to change my mind. That they're accepting of gay people and gay marriage is axiomatic – they're aged 16, 20, 24, and 25 – and, whether you like it or not, that generation in the west simply does not comprehend opposition on these issues.

As for pressure, you clearly don't know me. I have never compromised because of intimidation, even when it comes from genuinely violent and serious people. It's tragic but indicative that there are critics who cannot come to terms with growth and change and rather than considering what I have to say try to question my motives.

"No, I have evolved on this single subject because I can no longer hide behind comfortable banalities, have realized that love triumphs judgement, and know that the conversation between Christians and gays has to transform – just as, to a large extent, the conversation between conservatives and gays. I am not prepared to throw around ugly terms like 'sin' and 'disordered' as if they were clumsy cudgels, not prepared to marginalize people and groups who often lead more moral lives than I do, am sick and tired of defining the word of God by a single and not even particularly important subject. If we live we grow. The alternative is, of course, death."[3]

I am not naïve and have no sugary illusions about human nature but I had no idea of the effect the column would have. Remember, the article does not even mention gay marriage, let alone support it. Nor does it explicitly affirm same-sex relationships or any of the aspirations of the gay community. All it does is to call for a different, kinder, and if you like more Christian dialogue and to apologize for any harm or hurt caused. In some ways it was even a touch cowardly. That, however, seemed to be enough for what I can only describe as those old gates of the hot, burning place with the chap in red tights running around with a pitchfork to open wide. First came the abuse. I received more than a thousand e-mails, tweets, or Facebook comments alleging that I was a liar, a fraud, a pervert and that my gay lover was threatening to out me unless I publicly supported same-sex marriage. A private photograph of me in a rehearsed joke sketch in which I give the finger to a friend as he mocks me was stolen from a file and spread over the Internet alleging that it had happened live on television and was actually of me insulting people who were Catholic or were opposed to marriage equality. That photo, by the way, is still all over the Web and being used to attack me, and I am sure will be again when my enemies read this book. Those Christians using it should realize that theft is a sin – it was, as I say, stolen from a private collection – and that lying is also against the commandments. A conservative Roman Catholic blog, Contra|Diction, gave me perhaps my best headline ever with "Michael Coren Complicit in Destruction of Souls Who Practice Homosexuality, Pt 1."[4] No doubt there will be a sequel. I was accused of being an adulterer, and the editor of a newspaper for which I wrote a column – they later fired me – received a dozen calls and e-mails confirming that I was having an affair and that my poor wife had to be told. He called me, knew the slanders were baseless, and was outraged at the attacks. I told him that I was far too ugly to have an affair. While I laughed and still laugh at this particular attack, which was to be repeated countless times, it's worth wondering what could have happened if my wife and I had not had such a close and loving relationship or if our children had been younger and had heard these rumours.

I was compared to a pedophile and a child killer, it was alleged that one of my daughters – we never quite confirmed which of the two – was gay and that photos of her in "lesbian embraces" had recently been removed from her Facebook page. As it happens, both girls are straight, but this attack was especially odious as it targeted young people who were in no way involved in any of what was going on.

As vitriolic and openly hateful and menacing as such attacks were and continue to be, it is often the "compassionate" criticism that feels most hideous: those that do so in the form of sympathy and with partial explanations of why I have become a heretic and should go to hell. That self-righteous, ostensibly caring manner that was soon to become so achingly familiar to me is here typified by the leader of a Catholic group to which I had spoken on more than a dozen occasions:

> As your friend and brother in Christ, I am contacting you out of love to discuss a concern that has arisen. This is not easy, but Scripture calls me to contact you to discuss this sensitive topic. It has come to my attention that many Catholics are concerned with the video we saw of your program regarding the homosexual charity story. We are not sure what your beliefs are on the issues of homosexuality, and gay "marriage", as it relates to Catholic/Jesus' teaching? Can you please clarify? You have always been such a clear, bold voice for Catholic truth through your books and speeches for some time, but many in the Church are now concerned with these recent statements. It's hard for many of us to tell if you were affirming the gay life style. We are hoping you were merely trying to emphasize that all people – whether living in sin or not – should have a desire to help the orphaned, poor, hungry, etc.
>
> Given how articulate you are, we don't understand the ambiguity on this important moral area. Michael, as your brother in Christ, will you please reply to clarify your beliefs on this issue? God bless you and your family. You remain in my prayers, and please pray for me and my family, as well.

What he didn't say was that in my speeches to his organization's various branches across North America from New Orleans to Rhode Island and Indiana to Nebraska, I generally didn't discuss sexuality or gay themes at all and never, ever made it a key issue. A few days later, I received a note from Cardinal Collins, the Archbishop of Toronto. He's a kind and good man who cares for others and we had met for breakfast several times in the past two years but always at my request – he had never asked me to meet him. He's a very busy man and why would or should he? So this e-mail was extremely unusual. It transpired that he had received an inquiry, a complaint, concerning my stance on the issue of homosexuality. We met for breakfast, and the cardinal was his usual gentle self. Mostly we spoke about Catholic education but then he explained that he had been "sent a video from your nightly television show the *Agenda*" – I reminded him that my show was actually called *The Arena* – and that he was uncomfortable with it. We chatted, and while he didn't seem to listen very much to what I said, he did say that he was concerned with the terms "gay and gay community," preferred "people with same-sex attractions," but appreciated that I had to "speak quickly on television." I tried to explain that I had been struggling with the central mercy of the Gospel message for some time and how I could apply this to loving same-sex couples but my explanation didn't seem to be moving the conversation forward in any way. This exchange seemed entirely pointless. I have a feeling that both of us had already made up our minds. What surprised me was that a complaint or two about this particular issue should have caused him for the first time to initiate a meeting. I have not heard from the cardinal since that breakfast but I have certainly heard from many other critics.

Suddenly my speeches to Catholic and other Christian groups were being cancelled; conservative Catholic and right-wing Christian websites listed the contact details for my speeches and the names and e-mail addresses of my various editors and demanded that people write and telephone to have me cancelled and fired. Some of them recommended concerted campaigns in which people from different provinces, states, and even countries made contact at different times so as to make the opposition appear more extensive and broad-based than it might otherwise seem and, as a consequence, to inflict the greatest damage. As with my children, my Facebook and Twitter accounts were analyzed and certain comments taken out of context and repeated to prove that I was a very bad man indeed. I was called a "homo-fascist," it was alleged that a former employer had fired me because I was mentally ill, that I had had a stroke, a brain tumour and was bi-polar. Not that I should have to say it, and anyway it's irrelevant, but none of these comments are true. Quite clearly some of these attacks came from the usual suspects – every group and cause has its fanatics. Read the comments section beneath almost any on-line newspaper column and you will see the sewers breathe, before your very eyes.

I'm hardly naïve about the venom possible in such matters, especially on such a hot-button issue, and most especially coming from true believers who feel they have God on their side. However, what did surprise me was the sheer number of people involved, that they called themselves Christians, and that some of them were ordained Catholic priests and Protestant ministers as well as lawyers, academics, and teachers. This was not just the usual gang but those with graduate degrees, those who have sworn to love God, those who actually know me and my family.

Yet the more I was attacked the more I saw the hypocrisy of those who claimed to be loving, and as a consequence the more firm I became in defending and speaking up for the gay community. Let me emphasize that I do not accuse all opponents of equal marriage of being cruel and dishonest – I know many of them to be kind, good people – but within the organized church-based opposition to the gay community and equal marriage there is in my experience something worryingly dark and dangerous going on. It reminded me of what the Anglican priest, author, and broadcaster Mark Oakley said when he used an image with its origins in the Methodist community and wrote of the dangers of "the swimming pool Church – one that has all the noise coming from the shallow end. In such a paddling pool it will be easy to say 'easy' and mysterious to say 'mysterious' . . . a Church more interested in self-indulgence, imposed boundaries and small interest groups. It will be fearful of truthful and genuine debate and will lack the confidence to form friendships."[5] In my case, however, this particular part of the pool wasn't shallow but positively empty, and those standing in it seemed to want to push me into the deep end with heavy weights around my neck and hope and pray – especially pray – that I couldn't swim.

This self-indulgence, noise, and fear lead inevitably to cruelty and panic, which is precisely the opposite of the Christian message. For example, I received dozens of graphic accounts of sexually transmitted diseases, sometimes with quite horrible illustrations, and was told ludicrously that these were the virtual preserve of gay people. Beyond AIDS, I was told of all sorts of illnesses, diseases, wounds, and disorders that were rife within the gay community. I was such a fool, they told me, I needed to learn and understand before it was too late. Lesbianism seldom seemed to figure in these letters, and there was a strange, bewildering but perhaps revealing obsession with anal sex, not to mention a near total lack of understanding of the realities of gay life. Perhaps this was understandable but their tangible hatred was not. They hadn't even made an attempt to think outside of a gruesome and malignant stereotype and one that leads to incalculable pain, suffering, and discrimination.

At around the same time as this was happening, we debated on my television show the decision of American football player Michael Sam to announce that he was gay. One of my guests, a British-educated but Toronto-based evangelical pastor named Joe Boot who has written several books and is building an international reputation, disagreed with Sam for numerous reasons. I argued that we must not allow zealots to define and decide the debate or the language of discourse. The Reverend Boot disagreed and insisted on using the words *sodomy* and *sodomite*. I said that he was being deliberately offensive, that it was absurdly reductive to distill gay relationships to a single sexual act, that the language was archaic and by its nature pejorative, that half of the gay community were women, and that many gay men might not even consider this activity as part of their relationship. I also argued that gay people do not choose their sexuality and that we must appreciate the love and affection that exists between gay men and women. Also, do we describe heterosexual couples merely by the act of sexual intercourse? Of course not. My guest disagreed with me on all these issues. This interview, as with the one concerning Uganda and the idea of imposing the death penalty for homosexuality, also went viral and led to another wave of attacks.

I was repeatedly accused of giving in to pressure or, more often, of changing my opinion because I wanted to make money. Reluctant as I am to discuss money, I have lost at least half of my income because of my reformed position on gay issues. If this was about making cash, I've got it all terribly wrong. There also seems to be a belief among opponents of gay equality that the gay community is supernaturally powerful and influential and will suddenly reward people who support them and, naturally, punish those who oppose them. It's a little similar to the rantings of anti-Semites who are convinced that Jews control the world and its finances and that we oppose them at our peril and become overnight millionaires if we embrace the cause. There was no pressure, there is no money, and there is no hidden agenda. It's especially ironic in that the same conservative Christians who were so intent on "exposing" me and making my life so difficult tend to be the first to complain that they are being persecuted for opposing gay rights.

Another method of attack was to dismiss me and my views as, apparently, I was always changing my mind and changing my religion. One person wrote to me, "You were a Jew, then a Catholic, now you're a gay." I'm not sure what denomination "gay" is but the truth is that although my father was Jewish, I was not raised with any religion at all. I became a Christian in 1984 and have remained a Christian ever since. In that period, I did leave the Catholic Church for a few years in the late 1990s to worship in a number of different Christian churches, partly because I was speaking in these churches at least every second week, but then returned. But that was the only real change. I have never moved an inch from orthodox Christian teaching in thirty-two years. I do now worship as an Anglo-Catholic in the Anglican Communion but that's partly because I couldn't in all integrity and with respect toward the Roman Catholic Church continue to receive its sacraments while knowing in my heart that I disagreed with some of its social and moral teachings. One would have thought that Catholics would have at least understood this but that was certainly not the response I experienced. Knowing how many Catholics do receive the sacraments while rejecting Catholic teaching and knowing that some of those people were now attacking me was, I must admit, sometimes difficult to take. As for changing my mind "all the time," the truth is that I have been boringly consistent over the years. But anyway, I have never understood why learning, evolving, growing, and changing is thought to be such a bad thing, especially from a spiritual and religious point of view. Perhaps I am taking it too personally and even over-thinking it, when what it amounts to is merely another way to try to discredit me, to discredit my views, and to discredit the gay community.

The amount of time and space devoted to me was, I suppose, paradoxically flattering but also incredibly surprising. One traditionalist Catholic blog ended an extensive diatribe about me with a large picture of a corpse hanging from a tree. Another tried in some obscure way to connect my change of view on equal marriage to the tragic, macabre, and infamous rape and murder by three gay men of a twelve-year-old shoeshine boy in Toronto in 1977. Another fellow spent an admirable amount of time creating pictures of me surrounded by naked men at various Pride parades from around the world. There was I, smiling at the camera for a portrait shot, with the caption in quotes that "gay people are the finest Christians." What I had actually said was, "After so much persecution, stigma, and pain, those gay men and women who have remained Christian are some of the finest Christians I have ever met." Almost every word was juxtaposed with a naked bum or a blushingly visible penis. It's noticeable how often a Pride parade composed of hundreds of thousands or even a million people is characterized by opponents, and even some supporters, by the few dozen men and women who wish to walk around naked. I'm not at all supportive of such behaviour and I know many gay people agree with me. In fact the Grand Marshal of one of the largest Pride parades in the world told me that if he could he would remove all nudity from the event. He also stressed that the church groups in the parade massively outnumbered the naked marchers. I was advised on several occasions by friends who were lawyers that I should sue some of the people writing about me. I chose not to, partly because it would only give them and their cause more publicity and also because unlike most of the self-professed Christians attacking me, I do believe in turning the cheek and forgiving when at all possible. But, my God, there were times when it was extremely difficult to do so.

I also received hundreds of notes from people, both gay and straight, thanking me for what I had said and written. I was surprised and delighted by how forgiving and encouraging so many gay people were and also by how little cynicism there was and how rare were those who dismissed me as someone who had waited for far too long to come around to their way of thinking. Some of the letters brought me to tears with their stories of personal suffering, pain, and loss, and I have made many friends and learned a great deal through all of this. I also received letters from reasonable critics who made quiet, calm arguments but, in all honesty, these were not numerous. There were also those – including two senior Roman Catholic priests – who wrote to me and, while I knew them to disagree with me, said simply that our friendship was lasting and solid and that no more had to be said. But it would be dishonest to say that all of this made the attack campaign irrelevant. It hurt, it stung, and it scarred. Yes, I know that Friedrich Nietzsche said, "That which does not kill us makes us stronger" but he was dead at fifty-five and I had just turned fifty-six. The whole experience boosted my empathy, deepened my faith, and gave me a vision and a perspective that I had not previously possessed but it also left a mark and one that, if I am candid, has yet to heal. Perhaps, however, that is for the best.

Around the time of my conversion on the issue of same-sex marriage, I published a book about the persecution of Christians by Islamic fundamentalists. It had nothing whatsoever to do with homosexuality or any sexuality at all for that matter. It was exclusively about the persecution and slaughter of Christians in Muslim-majority nations, perhaps the darkest example of religion-based attacks since the Holocaust. I had worked extensively on the subject, travelling widely and speaking to Christians from Pakistan, Egypt, Iraq, Syria, Iran, and much of the Muslim world. Their stories were heartbreaking, and I was anxious to tell of such pain to any and every audience whatever their faith, politics, nationality, or sexuality. It mattered. I did a lot of media for the book, and I had always been invited onto a radio show called *Catholic Answers* to discuss my various books or even columns. This time, however, the producers failed to respond to repeated e-mails, which had never happened before. The book's subject was, after all, exactly what the listeners to *Catholic Answers* were interested in, and ISIL and the Middle East were in the news every week. After a fourth or fifth e-mail I did receive a response from Patrick Coffin, the host and producer of *Catholic Answers*:

"Okay, deep breath. There's no soft way to say this, and it wasn't my decision. Hear me out because I'm writing as a true admirer of yours, and – I trust it's mutual – a friend. There is enough consternation and head scratching among the senior staff at *Catholic Answers* over your apparent change of heart on the matter of homosexuality that we're going to wait before having you back on. Your books as well, for now, are no longer sold on our website. I'm just confused. In the first column, the reason you give for your change of heart (new realization and empathy) is the reaction you got from some people to your defense of human rights for persecuted homosexuals in Russia and Africa. You also never really say what you were wrong about, exactly. That you regret using words like sin and disordered? It made me wonder if you would endorse using them if they didn't sound like clumsy cudgels. A reasonably intelligent reader could conclude that you don't believe same-sex attractions are objectively disordered. I could do a line-by-line Q&A on your column, which is uncharacteristically mushy and illogical; not the time or place. . . . It appears that you have, at best, made peace with a newly popular form of highly ambiguous, wink-and-nod language about homosexuality, or, at worst, rejected Catholic teaching altogether. It's impossible to tell from your columns. The homophile movement within the Catholic Church (by which I mean otherwise orthodox, pro-chastity Catholic writers who self-identify as 'gay and Catholic' and who take for granted that same-sex attractions are some kind of special gift to humanity) has its converts here and there. In some ways, I can understand why. But it simply can't be squared with an authentic Catholic anthropology. I believe there is a way to be kind, and respectful and good-natured and open to dialogue – while maintaining a solid conviction that same-sex behavior is a very bad thing for the human person as loved so well by God. There are very good reasons why magisterial documents (not to mention sacred scripture) don't use terms like gay and lesbian. For one, they are chiefly tribal identity markers that assume same sex attractions to be either natural/good, or permanent; and they presuppose that grounding one's identity in immoral sexual behavior is a good thing."

What intrigued me most about the letter was that the book I wanted to discuss was about the persecution of Christians and at no point would we be discussing homosexuality. It's an incredibly important subject and one that screams out for further discussion. The people at *Catholic Answers* must have known this, Patrick Coffin must have known this. Yet more important, it seemed, than speaking up for slaughtered Christians was making sure that a man who wanted to be gracious to gay men and women was not allowed to speak about any issue at all. I have no doubt whatsoever that only a few months earlier I would have been welcomed on the show. This was not to be the last such letter.

Others were positively extraordinary. "I have to wonder if you, Michael Coren might be suffering from what exorcists call demonic obsession. These are cases in which God permits the devil to torture a person with repetitive thoughts that the person cannot control. Another possibility is something in your personal life that has created cognitive dissonance. For example, if you had a relative who revealed an addiction to sodomy, Michael Coren, you might not have the intellectual capacity to understand that the teaching of the Church is mercy and grace for that person. In this case, his whole apostasy would be a misguided attempt to protect yourself from the knowledge that someone he loves is on the way to hell."

I began to block people on Facebook and Twitter who appeared to spend hours, days, weeks writing to me and about me but they still managed to get through. To be candid, sometimes I couldn't resist looking at their comments and postings, much against the advice of my far more phlegmatic wife – who herself was mentioned quite a lot as the victim in all this and as someone who had to be prayed for because it couldn't be easy being married to someone who supported "sodomite unions." Nor am I speaking of a dozen or few dozen crazies here but several hundred people and entire groups and organizations all over the English-speaking world. I know for a fact that some of my attackers attended the same church as my wife and knew where I lived and were aware of some of the details of my family life. There is none so angry as a fundamentalist scorned, as I discovered time and time again. Conservative Catholics and evangelicals assumed I was critical of them for not being sufficiently liberal when in fact I was critical of them for not being sufficiently Christian. In fact, it is not the Christian fervour but the lack of it that is so distressing about so many socially conservative Christians.

More serious in many ways than the personal attacks were the attacks on my livelihood. Beyond the firings and silencing in Catholic circles, the evangelical world now became involved. For more than twelve years, until 2009, I had hosted a nightly show on Crossroads Television. I had won numerous awards for the network and interviewed prime ministers, celebrities, famous authors, and hundreds of politicians and personalities who would not otherwise have ever appeared on a program broadcast from a Christian network. In 2015, I began to appear as a co-host on *100 Huntley Street*, the flagship of the network. For a full week, I appeared and conducted a number of interviews about faith and science, the Armenian genocide, ISIL, education, and various other issues – never, though, about homosexuality. I was then booked to record more interviews. I spoke to the producers at *100 Huntley* about my position on the gay issue and told them that out of respect to them I would not discuss it on air. They were satisfied and told me that I was "far more of an asset than a liability." Then just a few days before the confirmed dates for my next interviews, I received an e-mail from executive producer George McEachern:

"I trust this email finds you well. This is a difficult conversation that I need to have with you. It is felt that with the high public profile you have in media and social networking in relation to gay marriage and the Catholic Church it is felt that we have to part our ways as an organization. I know that you had mentioned earlier that you understood if this would be the case. I believe God was informing you back then what we would be hearing from our partner base as well as our evangelical community. You were right. Michael I wish there was another means beyond *Huntley* that we could walk alongside of you. I believe you are a professional and a Christian with strong convictions. I know that in my heart. I think for myself being a member of the United Church of Canada gives me a better understanding of what you had been wrestling with. I do pray that the Lord will lead and guide your ways and provide for you and family. Although this is a departure for us professionally, I trust that we can keep a personal friendship alive. Thank you for understanding and keep well my friend."

It has always fascinated me how when I am being fired or insulted, so many conservative Christians explain how they are praying for me. What made this particular case so difficult to accept was that in February 2013 I had publicly defended

*100 Huntley Street* in print and on air when it had been accused of homophobia and was in danger of losing some government funding when it was revealed that its website had carried a list of what were referred to as "sexual sins" considered to be "perversions." The site spoke of "turning from the true and/or proper purpose of sexual intercourse; misusing or abusing it, such as in pedophilia, homosexuality and lesbianism, sadism, masochism, transvestism, and bestiality." It asked people to repent and said that "God cares too much for you (and all of His children) to leave such tampering and spiritual abuse unpunished." The management at Crossroads immediately removed the acid statements and explained that they didn't even know they were there and that they had been cut and pasted from another site much earlier and without their knowledge. It didn't speak well of their professionalism but I had never considered those who worked at Crossroads to be hateful. Thus I defended them loudly and with conviction and I think it did quite a lot of good. Alas, that defence was not reciprocated. I was now banned from Crossroads television not for what I had said on its programs but because of what I thought and what I had said and written elsewhere.

This was also the time when cake became tasty. Mind you, it's always been. But in this case it was media tasty because in a series of actually quite bizarre cases various gay couples were told by Christian bakers that they had to buy their wedding cakes elsewhere. Let them eat cake, but whatever you do, don't actually bake it for them. The more I saw conservative Christian confectioners, wedding dress store owners, or florists proclaim their faith as the reason for refusing to provide services to same-sex couples, the more I asked myself – and my readers – if these devout people had ever refused service to heterosexual couples who are divorced or who are living together. Jesus has quite a bit to say about those issues but nothing about homosexuality. It's worth remembering that for many years people refused to serve interracial couples and often used their interpretation of their Christian faith as the reason. It also became obvious that the entire issue of withholding service to gay people and gay couples has suddenly become to some a cause of freedom and free speech. But many of these new zealots had said nothing up to that point when their opponents were silenced and certainly did not speak up for gay men and women who in the past had been denied basic liberties. Paranoia and the idea that a great persecution had started drenched the anti-gay movement and I was evidently seen as someone who had gone over to the persecuting side. It's all totally ridiculous, of course, but while there have been some cases in which people have suffered financially and personally because of their beliefs – albeit intolerant beliefs – most of the examples of alleged persecution turn out on further research to be political clashes where major funding from conservative Christian and political groups comes into play and the ostensible victims in the end do rather well. It's something I discuss at greater length later in the book. I mention it here because I was now seen as part of the problem whereas I had been championed as a star of the solution. Then there was the anti-Semitism. This was a minority report within the campaign but it was significant how often people described me as "a Jew" or "jew" – ostentatiously omitting the capital letter to indicate contempt. I was Coren the Jew who had turned on Christianity, Coren the Jew who was only in it for the money. No, only Coren the half-Jew in it for the money half the time.

None of this, of course, comes close to the experience of exclusion, marginalization, persecution, oppression, and violence inflicted on so many gay men and women for so very long, and I would never have the audacity to claim otherwise. But I have at least experienced a glimpse of the reality of all this. As a middle-aged, very white, very straight, very Christian man, I was obliged, first reluctantly and then eagerly, to explore the complex dynamic between faith and homosexuality and to work out a new narrative. The crux of that narrative: God is love. The love I felt when I first saw my newborn children, when I watched my mother dissolve into Alzheimer's, when I found my late father's diaries that spoke of his pride in our family, when I feel closest to the Christ I worship. Jesus spoke of love for everybody and called for forgiveness, justice, truth, turning the other cheek. As my faith has deepened over the years, I have tried to broaden the circle of inclusive love rather than guard the borders of what I once thought was Christian truth. Instead of holding the door firmly closed, I want to hold it wide open. I have realized that Christianity is a permanent revolution, a state of being in which we believers must challenge our preconceptions every moment of every day. How dare I – with all my brokenness and sordid, banal sinfulness – criticize someone simply because he or she wants to live life fully? How the hell dare I? The standard Christian response to homosexuality is the familiar but entirely inadequate mantra "love the sinner but hate the sin." In other words, a gay person's sexual and romantic attractions – much of their being and personality, and all that they want in a lasting relationship – is sinful, but they themselves are just fine. By way of analogy, the teachings go, Christians love alcoholics but not alcoholism, love those who commit adultery but not the act of adultery itself. Such logic presupposes that same-sex attraction is no more central to a person's identity than substance abuse or unfaithfulness – which any reasonable person knows to be untrue and, more to the point, is completely lacking in sensitivity and understanding and is also downright insulting.

More extreme Christians believe that one can pray away the gay and that gay people can be changed, which is why some continue to support so-called conversion therapy. It's a foolish and dangerous notion that I have never taken seriously even when I opposed equal marriage. They bristle at the suggestion that gays and lesbians are born that way because, if that thread of biological reasoning is accepted, it implies that God created people who are powerfully disposed toward what conservative Christians regard as sinful lifestyles and that is something they can never accept. The whole thing is like some theological rabbit hole that gets darker as you descend. It's also dishonest. As I mentioned earlier, I have spoken to hundreds of Catholic groups and parishes over the years, and I would estimate that one out of every three priests is gay, and by no means are they all celibate. (Others have put the number as high as 50 per cent, as we shall see later.) The joke at the Vatican is that if the Swiss Guard find a priest in bed with a man, they are to ignore it but if it's with a woman they have to report it at once. There's humour in that joke, but also horrifying hypocrisy. There are Catholic priests all over the world living with their partners and some of these men are prominent clerics. Living that lie, existing in such a state of moral dissonance, is achingly damaging. One former priest told me that he once visited a senior bishop (I am being purposely vague here and will not name him) to explain that he was gay and needed to leave the priesthood. The bishop responded that it was okay and that if every gay priest left his diocese there would be hardly anybody left. He then told the priest that he himself was gay and listed various other senior clerics who were homosexual, some of whom he had had relationships with. What an absurd state of affairs in the twenty-first century.

Evangelical denominations have a far less subtly embedded gay culture – in part because they permit their male clerics to marry women – but there are infamous cases of high-profile Protestant critics of homosexuality being outed. Their hypocrisy takes another form: most evangelical churches blithely will remarry divorced people (even ministers can be divorced), despite the fact that Jesus, who doesn't say a single word about homosexuality, is fiercely critical of dissolving a marriage. Indeed, in the Roman, Greek, and Jewish cultures in which he lived – where divorce was common and easy – his stance was revolutionary. Yet his followers have ignored those Christian teachings while inventing others on sexuality. When it comes to same-sex marriage, history is not on the side of the conservatives. Academics, popular historians, and theologians alike are re-exploring the context of Biblical passages and coming to a new understanding of what scripture says about homosexuality, a term not even invented until the nineteenth century. For me, though, the journey was first emotional and then academic and then theological. When I finally accepted the full inclusion of LGBT people into the Christian church, I felt a little like Ebenezer Scrooge on Christmas morning. It wasn't too late, I had been shown the world's possibilities, I could start again and afresh, make amends, try to put things right, follow Jesus Christ absolutely and not partially. Love triumphs over law, the words of the Son of God over those of the sons of Pharisees, and we shed a skin of fear and misunderstanding to put on the cloak of understanding and community.

In late 2014, I had lunch in downtown Toronto with the publisher of a leading gay Internet site. We talked shop, laughed, drank wine. Family came up, and I showed him some photographs of my wife and he remarked on her good looks. There was a long pause. He turned his phone around and showed me a picture of his husband. Then he looked up: "I was hesitant to show that to you. I was uncomfortable with how you might react." I felt ashamed and very small. "You know," he continued, "you had quite an effect on my life. I'd just come to Toronto – wasn't even out yet – and I was meeting with a colleague. He went off to the washroom, and I read the newspaper he had with him. It was the *Toronto Sun* and you had a column in it that was critical of gay people. Of me, really. It broke my heart." The two of us are friends now. Actually, I have lots of new friends. In the summer of 2015 I was asked to preach at Toronto's Metropolitan Community Church (MCC). MCC is not exclusively gay but its central theme, its charisma if you like, is outreach to LGBT people, and in all of its many international branches it is at the heart of the struggle for full equality. Indeed, in Toronto its leader, Brent Hawkes, is one of the most high-profile, visible, and eloquent leaders of the gay community. It was Brent who invited me to speak at the church – we had known each other for years because we often appeared on opposing sides on television and radio panels; neither of us ever thought we'd be embracing, close to tears, in front of the altar of his church. I'd spoken to hundreds of groups for more than a decade and hadn't felt nervous for a long time but was most definitely nervous this time. How many of these people had I hurt, how many had lives made more difficult by my writing and broadcasting? I'd never hated but I had given an intellectual veneer to the anti-gay movement, had enabled – even unintentionally – some muddy bigotry. Yes, I was nervous, and a little ashamed.

There were two services, with a combined congregation of around seven hundred men, women, and some children. And as I walked in on that hot, rainy morning, I was sensing no condemnation, no cynicism, no grudges. As an emotionally constipated Englishman, I was several times close to weeping as I witnessed a feeling of authentic Christian community that I have, with all due respect, not always found in mainstream church settings. I saw collectives of warmth and support, groups of people from various ethnicities, backgrounds, sexualities, and experiences united in acceptance. After so many months of abuse, accusations, and firings, my sense of liberation was exquisite. I told them that as a straight man who had reversed his position on gay rights and equal marriage, I had recently experienced a glimpse of a shadow of a whiff of what it must be like to be a gay Christian. I said that some of the finest Christians I had ever met had been people who were gay and had remained true to Jesus Christ. I said that remaining Christian in the face of hostility and even vitriol was an indication of an enormous depth of faith and was a living, fleshy example of a glorious mystery. I spoke of unconditional love, of what scripture actually said about sexuality rather than the popular and misguided caricature of Biblical truth that we are so often offered. I said that the only absolutes were grace and love. Never has a standing ovation felt so true, so good, and so pure.

My life now is very different from what it was. There are publications and places that will never again be open to me and that's a shame and something I deeply regret. Not because of the money but because we need to speak about all this and learn from one another. There are people who will never forgive me for what they see as a betrayal and that's a shame too but surely it is they who have to take that step forward. There are those who have been genuinely hurt because they respected my voice and thought I was once one of their own and spoke for them – and that's something that does concern me – but on so many issues I do still speak for them and believe that by this change I can communicate the Gospel to those who otherwise would never have listened. But I have also received many letters from gay people and the families of gay people that have broken my heart and simultaneously filled me with joy. The spirit of forgiveness and gratitude has astounded me and I have learned more than I thought possible from these men and women. More than this, once the door of the house spiritual is opened, the wind that blows through the various rooms is irresistible. I have had to rethink all sorts of things and I am a much better person because of it. My Christian faith, though, has only been made stronger. No more stones to be thrown.

Let me give you a parallel. The Christian church used to believe that suicide was so heinous that those who took their own lives were denied a Christian burial. Times, thank the Lord, have changed, and now even Roman Catholics offer prayers for the deceased, say Mass for them, and offer pity. The Catholic author and apologist G.K. Chesterton said, "Not only is suicide a sin, it is the sin. It is the ultimate and absolute evil, the refusal to take an interest in existence; the refusal to take the oath of loyalty to life. The man who kills a man, kills a man. The man who kills himself, kills all men. As far as he is concerned he wipes out the world." But while Chesterton could be incisive and brilliant, he could also be severe, self-consciously judgemental, and simply wrong. We can't fully understand the will to suicide because such pain is by its nature beyond the understanding of the mentally healthy person. But anyone who has spent time with, for example, the schizophrenic or the profoundly depressed can gain at least a glimpse of the hell that is mental illness. I remember a friend of ours sitting in our home and physically moving his head in reaction to noises he was hearing that had not actually occurred. They were as real to him as were his hands or his feet. In many ways mental illness is worse than most physical ailments. We know how to fix a broken limb or heal most diseases, but even when we know what obscures and scrambles the mind, we are often incapable of doing very much about it. A new generation of drugs has enabled psychiatrists and doctors but they still fight the battle terribly under-armed. From a Christian point of view, this is all deeply significant and has wider repercussions because it shows how a faith can grow as its followers learn and discover more about life's realities. In addition to scripture, reason, and tradition, there is also experience, science, and knowledge. Christianity is not some dead, lifeless ideology but a living, vibrant, growing belief system. Christians used to apply an understanding of the fifth commandment that allowed no exceptions for suicides because we did not know enough about mental illness and the very real suffering of those in the deep dungeon of depression. Now we do know, do understand, and the church has reformed itself accordingly. That, surely, is God's plan. To be faithful is not the same as being reactionary, to be orthodox is not the same as being angry, to be devout is not the same as obsessing about an iron certainty. The more we learn, the more we understand; the more we understand, the better we are; the better we are, the more Christian we can become. We know more about the reality of same-sex attraction, of genuine and committed love between people of the same gender than did the writers of the Old Testament or Saint Paul. If love is at the very centre of the Christian message, surely the more we feel and appreciate genuine love the closer we are to that Christian message. To obscure the gift as we argue about the packaging is to indulge in precisely what Jesus Christ told us to avoid and warned us would lead good people astray.

Perhaps the most memorable comment in all this came from my twenty-six-year-old daughter. "Oh Dad, I've always loved you and always admired and respected you and always would have whatever your views. But I am so, so pleased you've come to a different conclusion, come to the right conclusion." Such wisdom from one so young. She must have a very clever mum indeed.

I'm not going to pretend it's always been easy since I made my new beliefs public. I was given loving counsel by many people, found solace in prayer and the reading of Christian books and scripture, and felt increasingly that I was closer to God not only because of my embrace of love for all but also because of the attacks on me that were a consequence of this new attitude. Pain causes vulnerability and vulnerability leads to a need to look deeper within. In my case, it also obliged me to rethink and come to terms with my earlier life and sometimes to try to grasp the comfort, warmth, and certainty of child-hood and youth. I thought more of my good, tolerant, superbly ordinary parents and wondered how they would have reacted. I knew what they thought about it all: while equal marriage would have shocked them because of their generation and the era, their indefatigable sense of justice and equality would – did – lead them to accept, encourage, and, as they would say, live and let live. That phrase may sound prosaic but if more people, and in this case more Christians, adopted it, there would be a world revolution. I have been privileged to meet some of the finest and purest Christians in the world. They have inspired me and changed my life, but I think my Jewish but secular father embodied the spirit of love, forgiveness, sacrifice, and humanity more than anyone else I have ever encountered. He had never really been taught about Christianity, knew little about Christian beliefs, and was convinced that the sandpaper of self-righteousness had rubbed away much of the splendour of organized faith.

Phil Coren's attitude toward Christianity became acutely apparent at Christmas because, of course, while he didn't celebrate the actual religious festival, he lived its loving essence. When I was a little boy, the season for me began at around two on Christmas Day morning. That was when I heard the distinctive sounds of his London black cab diesel engine driving up the suburban east London street to our house. To a child, work means nothing. I didn't realize, and my father would have been angry if I had done, that he was not paid when he didn't work, but that whatever happened, he would always devote Christmas Day to his wife and children. So he worked fourteen hours on Christmas Eve. It was why he was always so sleepy when my sister and I ran into our parents' bedroom horribly early and screamed about Santa's generosity. Sometimes we almost resented Dad's tiredness. I wish I could hug him right now and weep my sorrow. I'm sure he would tell me not to worry about it.

My father had driven a cab for most of his working life, after his years in the RAF and time spent as a boxer. The armed forces, tough sport, and a rough upbringing had formed him into a hard but gentle and warm person. He told off-colour jokes, sometimes swore, spoke his mind. When I met the woman I would later marry, I proudly showed my dad a photograph of this gorgeous girl whose mother was born in India.

He agreed that she was beautiful but said, "A bit dark, isn't she." I shouted at him and stormed off. Ten minutes later he found me. "Mike, I'm an idiot. I'm sorry. I'm so sorry. I was wrong. Please forgive me." Not a human rights commission story, but a tale of blood-red reality. He was a product of his age and his environment and he had reacted rather than thought. But when forced to consider what he had said, justice trumped pride. Here was humility. We are not Oprah clones but broken people. What defines us is not pretending to be perfect but acknowledging when we're not.

In 1985 I was received into the Church. My dad's reaction was "Whatever makes you happy must be a good thing but don't tell me about it." But he was not a saccharine man. When I married my Catholic wife in a Catholic church, he said, "Mike, I love you, I'll do anything for you, but I can't come, I can't. It wouldn't feel right, I'd be a fraud." But he cashed in all his savings and gave the money to us to buy furniture for our rented apartment. Four months later when my wife and I went to Britain for Christmas, he'd made a note of all of the local Mass times for us.

Phil Coren died on August 14, in 2002. He had had a second stroke, was suffering from cancer, and had nursed my mum through Alzheimer's. It was not a good death, if any death can be described as such. Yet he'd never complained, never blamed anybody for his suffering, tried to make the best of it, and saw purpose in what was happening. The last time I saw him alive was when he came to visit us in Canada, and this time he came to church with the family and remained on his own while we went to receive the Eucharist. As I returned and sat down, I saw that he was crying. I held his arm and thanked God for a father who, more than so many people who boast belief, taught me about truth.

Oh, one last thing. When my father was in his late twenties, he and his good-looking, street-wise, confident friends went to parties, met girls, had fun, did all sorts of things that he never repeated to me. He had one particular friend named Billsy who travelled with the crowd but never seemed to quite fit in. They teased him a little, my father included. But they liked him and he seemed to like them and he was especially fond of my dad. One late night on the way home and after a few drinks, this quiet, slightly shy young man asked my father if he could speak to him alone and in confidence. They sat in a rather seedy all-night café and drank instant coffee. Billsy half-covered his face and told my dad in quiet and clearly embarrassed tones that he was "queer." My dad thought he was joking and laughed. The man didn't laugh back. My father then realized that this was serious and was worried that Billsy might be attracted to him. Billsy said it wasn't that at all. He had seen my father, he said, not as some potential partner but as someone he could trust. He was right. "I'll never forget what I said to him," my dad explained to me. "I told him I was surprised, even a bit shocked, but that it was how we treated other people and how we lived our lives that mattered and not whether we fell in love with or fancied men or women. I said I couldn't give a shit. Actually, I did care a bit if I'm honest but I knew I shouldn't. I never told anyone else because he asked me not to. We remained friends for a couple of years more and then we lost touch as young people do. I heard decades later from someone I met totally by chance, an old friend from the street where I grew up, that Billsy had died in the 1980s from AIDS. He'd done very well in life but he was too young to die. Not even sixty. Too young, too young. But I asked my old neighbour if he'd been happy and he said that he had been happy, very happy indeed. Then this man said to me, 'Did you know

he was gay? I had no idea, no idea at all. I bet you didn't either.'
I had to smile. I said that, yeah, I think I did have an inkling that
he might be. He'd had a good and happy life. That pleased me so
much. So much. Today, though, it would have been even happier
and he wouldn't have to pretend. I still don't understand it all
but thank God we live in better times. Those old days weren't
right, you know, not the way it should be. Billsy deserved better."
I hope and do believe my Jewish, God-ambiguous, working-
class, funny, tough, cynical, romantic, politically incorrect dad
would be very proud of me right now. A made-up mind is often
like a made-up bed. Very neat and tidy but there's nothing
actually in it.

# BIBLE BELIEVING

SINCE BECOMING A PUBLIC SUPPORTER of equal marriage and embracing the full acceptance of gay men and woman into the Christian church and the Christian community, I have been inundated with people trying to be helpful. God spare me from helpful people. These new acquaintances were so deeply concerned about my eternal soul that they wrote to me to explain that the Bible very clearly condemns homosexuality and, in fact, condemns homosexuality more than almost anything else. It's a baleful sin, I was reminded, crying out to Heaven for vengeance and I forgot that, to my lasting shame and peril. What they were actually referring to – even the Protestants – when they relished the "crying out to Heaven for vengeance" bit was a slice of Catholic moral theology that lists four sins doing the crying, the crimes including homicide; infanticide; fratricide; parricide; matricide; pride; gluttony; negligence of the poor; abuse of children; ignoring the cries of foreigners, widows, orphans, slaves, and the marginalized; and defrauding workers. Oh, and homosexual acts. Quite the list. The last, as we shall see, is a relatively recent interpretation of the sin of Sodom, but the rest of them are far more Biblical and ancient. Yet the funny thing is that I've seldom if ever received letters from conservative Christians complaining about how society treats migrants and refugees, about our lack of humility, about the worrying and increasing levels of gross over-eating, particularly in North America, or about the cutting back of support

49

payments to the poor or the exploitation of working people. At first I tried to reply to these letters and calls and even to reason with at least some of them, but it soon became depressingly and sometimes hilariously obvious that this was entirely pointless. For the most part, they weren't looking for discussion but for affirmation and were far more interested in condemning me than in considering what I had to say.

I sometimes think that if someone who had absolutely no familiarity with the Bible was suddenly exposed to the Christian world and its denizens, they would assume that large parts or even the bulk of the Old and New Testaments dealt with sex, homosexuality, abortion, and, in the case of some Christians, the merits of gun ownership and capitalism, the evils of vaccination, environmental activism, and liberalism. Try as I might I find very little in scripture about owning guns and nothing at all about medical inoculations. Flippancy aside, there's actually not much more in the Bible about homosexuality than there is about giving children an injection so that they don't die of routine diseases. It is hardly ever mentioned at all. In fact there are probably five or six mentions of what can loosely be described as same-sex relationships and attractions in the entire Bible and the most famous or infamous one, of course, is always mentioned whenever this issue is discussed in Christian circles. Homosexuality is in Biblical terms largely a non-issue and has been awarded a significance far beyond its status. Malcolm Johnson exposes this bewildering perversion of emphasis and double standard rather well in his book *Diary of a Gay Priest: The Tightrope Walker*: "It is condemned. It is expressly forbidden in Scripture. . . . Four General Councils forbid it, Luther and Zwingli weighed against it, and until recently it was distasteful to most people. What is it?

Lending money at interest."[1] In fact only a tiny fraction of the Bible is in any way related to same-sex relationships whereas more than 10 per cent is devoted to issues of economic inequality, exploitation, and injustice. From a literalist point of view, then, conservative evangelicals and right-wing Catholics are looking through the wrong end of the theological telescope and seeing the important themes as distant, blurred, black and white images and the insignificant in immaculate Blu-ray vision on seventy-inch plasma screens.

This is merely one chapter in one book and I am in no way claiming that what I say here is definitive about the subject. Nor do I and nor will I argue that anybody who reasonably or respectfully disagrees with me is a bigot or a hater when it comes to interpretation and understanding of scriptural references to homosexuality. I emphasize, however, the qualities of reason and respect, and, alas, my experience has been that these are not always as common as one would hope. The Bible is complex and often esoteric, and the more time we spend with it the more we realize this. It is generally those who think they've got it all figured out who seem to understand it the least. To believe that the Bible is opposed to or even forbids homosexuality is hardly an extreme or fanatical position, and for most of the history of the church it has been the dominant position. I simply happen to disagree, as do many other Christians as well as non-Christians and increasing numbers of theologians and scholars. What I do find objectionable is when this issue is exploited and abused as a litmus test and a means to measure one's faith and commitment to the truth and to Jesus Christ, when it is blown out of all proportion and used not as a starting point for dialogue but as a finishing post to decide who has passed the test and who has not.

From a personal point of view, I have seen this occur on numerous occasions; there are many out there who could tell stories of being dismissed from their jobs working for a church or at a Christian college or institution, not for theft, violence, criminality, refutation of doctrine, or even for being in a gay relationship but merely for suggesting that there is room in the Bible for the allowance of equal marriage and same-sex love. I would ask those who disagree with the entire premise of this book to stand back and consider for a moment the case of a committed, devout, honest, moral, loving Christian person fired from a church position or denied a post or a place at a Christian university merely because they had argued that on a minor subject within scripture and one that is mentioned a handful of times they disagreed with the status quo. I assure you that this has happened many times and is still occurring today – not in a theocracy or a dictatorship but in North America and Western Europe. So it's hardly a level playing field, hardly balanced, and, some of us would claim, hardly Christian.

But before we discuss what scripture actually says about the issue, we should briefly discuss how we are supposed to read and understand scripture in the first place. It is quite clearly wrong, anti-intellectual, crass, and downright dangerous to read any historical or even current document for that matter without understanding its context, purpose, setting, author, vocabulary, and style. If we take satire, parody, or caricature, for example, as being literally true, we get into all sorts of serious trouble. Words have meaning and meanings have words. Language is also mutable, and what particular words and language meant even a generation or two ago can be different from a contemporary understanding. So imagine the challenges and possible difficulty of understanding words written thousands of years ago in various languages. Then we have issues of translation and emphasis and scratching away to find the original meaning of a text. With the Bible this is even more complex because this is a sacred work containing stories and accounts that shape lives, cultures, nations, and souls. It matters very much indeed. We're speaking here of nuanced and multi-faceted books and stories, containing history, poetry, metaphor and truth, miracle and anecdote, guides on how to love and accounts of how others failed to live. It's also the case that we know more now about who wrote the scripture, why they wrote it, and what they meant by it than at any time since it was first read. Generations of Biblical archaeology, linguistic discoveries, and historical research have made us far more and not less knowledgeable about these ancient texts than in the past, and if we filter all of this through the modern prisms of contemporary science, sociology, and human understanding we are, in effect, the most equipped Biblical scholars in history.

On a less sophisticated but deliciously biting if naughty level, a letter has been doing the social media rounds for a few years that was written by someone – we're still not precisely sure who the original culprit was – in response to the extremely conservative and ostentatiously religious Dr. Laura Schlesinger. The radio host and general life-and-everything expert had repeatedly made negative remarks about homosexuality, same-sex relationships, and equal marriage and based much of what she said on Biblical precedent. She went so far as to refer to gays as "mistakes of nature" and at her peak spoke to an enormous and eager audience. She is not, by the way, a medical doctor. The letter is obviously a little contrived but it does make a certain point and makes it rather well.

"Dear Dr. Laura: Thank you for doing so much to educate people regarding God's Law. I have learned a great deal from your show, and try to share that knowledge with as many people as I can. When someone tries to defend the homosexual lifestyle, for example, I simply remind them that Leviticus 18:22 clearly states it to be an abomination . . . end of debate. I do need some advice from you, however, regarding some other elements of God's Laws and how to follow them.

"1) Leviticus 25:44 states that I may possess slaves, both male and female, provided they are purchased from neighbouring nations. A friend of mine claims that this applies to Mexicans, but not Canadians. Can you clarify? Why can't I own Canadians?

"2) I would like to sell my daughter into slavery, as sanctioned in Exodus 21:7. In this day and age, what do you think would be a fair price for her?

"3) I know that I am allowed no contact with a woman while she is in her period of menstrual unseemliness – Lev. 15: 19–24. The problem is how do I tell? I have tried asking, but most women take offence.

"4) When I burn a bull on the altar as a sacrifice, I know it creates a pleasing odor for the Lord – Lev. 1:9. The problem is my neighbours. They claim the odor is not pleasing to them. Should I smite them?

"5) I have a neighbour who insists on working on the Sabbath. Exodus 35:2 clearly states he should be put to death. Am I morally obligated to kill him myself, or should I ask the police to do it?

"6) A friend of mine feels that even though eating shellfish is an abomination – Lev. 11:10, it is a lesser abomination than homosexuality. I don't agree. Can you settle this? Are there 'degrees' of abomination?

"7) Lev. 21:20 states that I may not approach the altar of God if I have a defect in my sight. I have to admit that I wear reading glasses. Does my vision have to be 20/20, or is there some wiggle-room here?

"8) Most of my male friends get their hair trimmed, including the hair around their temples, even though this is expressly forbidden by Lev. 19:27. How should they die?

"9) I know from Lev. 11:6–8 that touching the skin of a dead pig makes me unclean, but may I still play football if I wear gloves?

"10) My uncle has a farm. He violates Lev. 19:19 by planting two different crops in the same field, as does his wife by wearing garments made of two different kinds of thread (cotton/polyester blend). He also tends to curse and blaspheme a lot. Is it really necessary that we go to all the trouble of getting the whole town together to stone them? Lev. 24:10–16. Couldn't we just burn them to death at a private family affair, like we do with people who sleep with their in-laws? (Lev. 20:14)

"I know you have studied these things extensively and thus enjoy considerable expertise in such matters, so I am confident you can help. Thank you again for reminding us that God's word is eternal and unchanging."[2]

Yes, of course it's not completely fair. But it's no less fair than what is routinely said by conservative Christians about equal marriage and less excessive than many of the things said by some of those same Christians about gay love, gay people, and gay aspirations that are ostensibly based purely on Biblical reference. One of the ironies, one of the imploding paradoxes of all this, is that the more fundamentalist and literalist that Christians become, the more they disagree about who has the correct understanding of scripture. Taking the Bible as literal truth without need of context and interpretation does not unite Christians but achieves the very opposite. Let's take the example of Canada, partly because that is where I live but also because it's a typical Western country with regard to its faith and churches. Canada has a relatively small evangelical community, around 10 per cent of the population, and that community is divided into numerous churches. Many Pentecostals, for example, would argue that unless someone has been given the gift of tongues, glossolalia, they were not fully and completely Christian in the purest sense. But even within Pentecostalism there are differences of opinion about this. Some evangelicals would argue that infant baptism – the theological stance of evangelical Anglicans, for example – is not a genuinely Christian concept and that only adult or believers' baptism constitutes a complete membership of the Christian community. But once again, there are many differences of opinions on this. Some would claim that no translation of the Bible other than the King James version is reliable for genuine Christian worship and that all others are inadequate. The list goes on. Within this ever-growing division of those who all claim to be guided and guarded by the same text, we only need to look at one particular sub-group, the Baptists, and ask if they all agree. Surely a fairly small denomination in a fairly small community, all of whom read the same translation of the same Bible, would agree on areas of profound significance? Not so. There are two main branches of the Baptist Church in Canada, not including the numerous breakaway churches, and although one of the two major groups ordains women, the other does not. This issue of deep and important theology and disagreement has led to splits, arguments, the leaving of churches, and sometimes an open hostility. Female ordination involves an understanding of the nature of God, the role and place of women in faith and society, the very essence of what the church is supposed to be. Yet it must be said that while this difference sometimes causes tension, both groups still regard each other as Christian and as Baptist. Such divisions are repeated throughout the world and in almost every denomination. There are hundreds of denominations and thousands of independent churches all convinced that their interpretation of scripture is the correct one. Beyond female ordination or infant baptism and beyond even evangelical theology, what of the nature of the Eucharist, papal authority, the existence of purgatory, salvation by faith alone, prayers for the dead, and so on and so on? Those issues and more separate Protestants from Catholics, and Catholics or at least Catholic teaching has the same reverence for sacred scripture as do evangelicals.

So there are two major conclusions we can draw from all this: one is that strict adherence to the Biblical text leads not to unanimity but to diversity of opinion and that while this causes a certain friction in the modern church the majority of these disagreeing Christians still regard one another as being within the pale of orthodoxy and as authentic followers of Christ. Yet if a Christian argues, with much evidence as we shall see, that the Bible is opaque and vague about homosexuality and even accepting of committed same-sex relationships, they are considered by countless other Christians to have abandoned the faith and are often condemned and persecuted. There are simply so many layers of double standards, inconsistency, and hypocrisy here. The second conclusion is that literalism tends to lead not to a more pristine grasp of God's truth but to self-defeating and even dangerous sectarianism. Regarding the dangers of the latter, in the 1980s the American stand-up comic

Emo Phillips wrote a joke that more than twenty years later was voted the funniest religious joke ever. Aside from the fact that voting for a joke is one of the least amusing notions imaginable, it does exemplify a certain danger implicit in the certainty that one's understanding of religious teachings and textual instruction is correct:

> Once I saw this guy on a bridge about to jump. I said, "Don't do it!' He said, "Nobody loves me." I said, "God loves you. Do you believe in God?"
>
> He said, "Yes." I said, "Are you a Christian or a Jew?" He said, "A Christian." I said, "Me, too! Protestant or Catholic?" He said, "Protestant." I said, "Me, too! What franchise?" He said, "Baptist." I said, "Me, too! Northern Baptist or Southern Baptist?" He said, "Northern Baptist." I said, "Me, too! Northern Conservative Baptist or Northern Liberal Baptist?"
>
> He said, "Northern Conservative Baptist." I said, "Me, too! Northern Conservative Baptist Great Lakes Region, or Northern Conservative Baptist Eastern Region?" He said, "Northern Conservative Baptist Great Lakes Region." I said, "Me, too! Northern Conservative Baptist Great Lakes Region Council of 1879, or Northern Conservative Baptist Great Lakes Region Council of 1912?" He said, "Northern Conservative Baptist Great Lakes Region Council of 1912." I said, "Die, heretic!" And I pushed him over.[3]

Today we can repeat jokes but not so long ago disagreement could have nasty and even fatal consequences. For some gay Christians, it still can be a very risky business. To make this personal, I believe that when Jesus broke bread and told His followers to eat it in memory of Him, it was meant literally, and I am convinced that this is the body and blood of Christ. Yet many good, sincere, and intelligent Christians disagree with me. I also believe that Mary, the Mother of Christ, has an elevated and important place in the Christian narrative and the story of salvation and that scripture teaches us that we need to honour her. Yet many good, sincere, and intelligent Christians disagree with me. These are matters capable of being questioned and, while vital and central, should also provide believers with room for respectful and affectionate dispute. These differences and many more that I haven't mentioned are far more significant than the few mentions of homosexuality in scripture but sometimes we wouldn't know it. There is so much, so very much, in these sacred texts that is open to discussion and that should be left to individual interpretation and the private conscience. It's belief in Christ that makes us Christian, not the gluing of prejudice to religious dogma. Iron insistence is the path of intolerance, inquisition, and persecution.

We can go further. The Christian understanding of the Bible and opinions on how to live and implement Biblical teachings also change with the times, and if this sounds convenient to the subject we're discussing or facile, we only have to apply it to any number of historical or even recent examples of church beliefs. I mentioned in the last chapter the example of how Christian attitudes toward suicide have changed but we could also speak of how non-Christians were once regarded, of the church's treatment of the Jews, of the separation of church and state, of issues of race and ethnicity, or of Catholic teaching about not just those who were not Christian but those who weren't Catholic. The death penalty, to take just one obvious example, is now opposed by many denominations and myriad

Christians but at one point was considered self-evidently just and completely legitimized by scripture. That same scripture is now used by Christians, including popes and archbishops, to oppose the very capital punishment that their predecessors once advocated. Obviously we are shaped by the age in which we live, and our faith, or at least certain manifestations of that faith, is no exception; those manifestations of faith include the Christian understanding of human nature and sexuality. If we take the case of procreation and birth control, until as recently as 1930 the Church of England opposed all artificial contraception but now the very idea of the church forbidding the use of condoms or the Pill would be unthinkable to Anglicans. Similarly with evangelicals, while the majority is still strongly opposed to abortion, most accept not only the need but the morality of contraceptives. Christians, even conservative Christians, have changed their thinking without having changed their Bible. While we can coat all of this in theological and philosophical colours, the truth is more monochrome. In the past they sometimes got it wrong.

Take the viscerally troubling subject of slavery, one that has social and racial repercussions that trouble society even today. Slavery has always existed in human history in various forms but the European, white enslavement of enormous numbers of men and women from Africa began in the sixteenth century and reached a highly lucrative and obscene peak in the eighteenth century and first half of the nineteenth century. The abolitionist movement was led by Christians, usually evangelical and Quaker, and we cannot fully understand the work of William Wilberforce, Thomas Clarkson, John Newton, and the rest without realizing that they were motivated and mobilized by a powerful Christian revulsion at slavery based on their reading of the Bible. Without Christian men and women moved to passion and anger by the sin of slavery, the trade would have continued for far longer. But while many of the defenders of slavery were unconcerned with religion and were driven by profit or indifference, many in the pro-slavery camp were Bible-believing Christians and felt justified in their defence of the indefensible by their approach to scripture. They pointed to Abraham's owning of slaves, to Canaan being made a slave to his brothers, to the Ten Commandments demonstrating an implicit acceptance of slavery by mentioning it twice, to Jesus not referring to it even though it was widespread in the Roman Empire, to St. Paul telling slaves to obey their masters and what he writes about the subject in the Epistle to Philemon. They added that slavery removed peoples from non-Christian, pagan cultures to countries where they could hear the Gospel, that just as women were commanded in scripture to play a subordinate role to men, slaves are also part of a precise social order. They argued that Christians were obliged to obey the civil government and that followers of Jesus should not mix faith with politics – that one is still used today but usually out of convenience when it suits the person repeating it. We may cringe when we read this today but as late as the 1860s these feelings were fairly common among conservative Christians and were all based on a strict reading of scripture. Jefferson Davis, president of the Confederacy, spoke for many God-fearing people when he said that slavery "was established by decree of Almighty God. . . . It is sanctioned in the Bible, in both Testaments, from Genesis to Revelation. . . . It has existed in all ages, has been found among the people of the highest civilization, and in nations of the highest proficiency in the arts." Alexander Campbell was one of the leading preachers and ministers of the age and one of the senior evangelicals of the time. He wrote, "There is not one verse in the Bible inhibiting slavery, but many regulating it. It is not then, we conclude, immoral." But, we would argue today, they were choosing specific passages of the Bible out of context and in isolation to satisfy their own agendas, and rather than applying the love of Christ they were incarcerated by the legalism of those He directly opposed. Quite so, and it seems pretty obvious when we look back at groaning examples from the past.

The Bible has to be read and understood intelligently and as the document it is and is supposed to be and not as a guidebook or manifesto to be twisted into various shapes to satisfy a pre-existing social and political way of thinking. The term *cafeteria Christian* is often thrown at those of us who believe we have to use the prism of thought, context, and current knowledge to understand scripture but if anyone is picking only certain dishes from the theological menu so as to satisfy their own particular appetite, it is surely those who feast on the minor elements of the Bible while avoiding the meat and potatoes – and, frankly, most of the side dishes, pudding, vegetables, and dip. Alan Wilson, Bishop of Buckingham, made this point rather well when writing in the *Guardian* in October 2014 in response to those of his fellow Christians who argued that the Bible showed quite clearly what marriage was and what it wasn't.

> Generally speaking, Old Testament marriage customs and mores reflect the social mores of the people in the story. Adam and Eve sound like the original simple nuclear family, one plus one for life. In a way, that was all they could be, since they were the only two people in the world at the time.

In Genesis 38, Levirate marriage comes on the scene. This is the involuntary marriage of a man to his brother's widow in order to continue the line. This kind of marriage was still theoretically current enough in Jesus's day for it to be the basis of a question the Sadducees asked him about a bride, seven brothers and resurrection (Matthew 22:23–32).

Deuteronomy institutes another involuntary form of marriage. A virgin automatically becomes the wife of her rapist, who is then required to pay the victim's father 50 shekels for the loss of his property rights. Unlike other Old Testament marriages, these are held to be indissoluble.

In Numbers 31:17–18 we find another form of involuntary marriage. A male soldier is entitled to take as many virgins as he likes for his wives from among his booty, but must kill his other prisoners. In Deuteronomy 21:11–14, marriage is made by selecting a beautiful woman from among the spoils of war, shaving her head and paring her nails. These marriages are dissoluble if she fails to please, but the woman is no longer saleable. Throughout much of the Old Testament, marriage does not require sexual exclusivity. Concubines are allowed, alongside wives. Abraham had only two concubines, where Solomon had 300, along with his 700 wives.

The basic principle of these relationships is that if a woman's father pays a man to take her away, she is his wife. If he pays her father to take her away, she is his concubine.

None of these arrangements, except perhaps that enjoyed by Adam and Eve, would be recognized as marriage today. Pretending that the church's present stance is biblical is not going to fool anyone who doesn't want to be fooled, and fewer and fewer people do.[4]

In other words, be extremely careful in what and how you argue against equal marriage when you try to do so by using the Bible alone because it could backfire dramatically. As I mentioned briefly in the chapter about my personal experience with embracing a new, different view of Christianity and its relationship with homosexuality, the conservative Christian confusion of emphasis can be baffling at times, and this is made abundantly clear when we look at how contemporary Christianity regards divorce. I make no apologies for using this juxtaposition more than once in the book because it is so deeply revealing about an error of judgement. In Matthew 16, Jesus is asked by a group of Pharisees whether divorce is lawful. He replies, "A man will leave his father and mother and be united to his wife, and the two will become one flesh. . . . So they are no longer two, but one flesh. Therefore what God has joined together, let no one separate." They then ask for clarification of how Moses treated divorce and Jesus replies, "Moses permitted you to divorce your wives because your hearts were hard. But it was not this way from the beginning. I tell you that anyone who divorces his wife, except for sexual immorality, and marries another woman commits adultery."

In Luke 16:18 Jesus says, "Everyone who divorces his wife and marries another commits adultery, and he who marries a woman divorced from her husband commits adultery"; in Matthew 5:32 He says, "But I say to you that everyone who divorces his wife, except on the ground of sexual immorality, makes her commit adultery, and whoever marries a divorced woman commits adultery"; in Mark 10:12, "And if she divorces her husband and marries another, she commits adultery"; and the references could continue. In other words, Jesus really does have an awful lot to say about divorce and, boy, is He against it. St. Paul follows suit several times. In his letter to the Romans, 7:1–3, he writes: "Do you not know, brethren – for I am speaking to those who know the law – that the law is binding on a person only during his life? Thus a married woman is bound by law to her husband as long as he lives; but if her husband dies she is discharged from the law concerning the husband. Accordingly, she will be called an adulteress if she lives with another man while her husband is alive. But if her husband dies she is free from that law, and if she marries another man she is not an adulteress."

So there we have it. Jesus condemned divorce. Often, loudly, and clearly. He also did so in a culture and an environment that was surprisingly open to divorce but gave women very few rights when marriages did come to an end. Nor was this confined to the Roman and Greek world – it was very much the case within first-century Judaism as well. Jesus was a revolutionary in what He said about divorce and would have alienated many of His listeners and followers and made Himself extremely unpopular with those who would have otherwise followed Him. But He refused to compromise, and there is no ambiguity about what He said at all. Yet most Protestants have allowed divorce for many years and many denominations have moved with social trends; they have tended to change with the times. The majority of evangelical churches would say not a word about congregants being divorced, even more than once. Indeed, there are leading clergy and evangelists who are divorced and remarried and their behaviour is considered entirely acceptable. The Roman Catholic Church has a stricter approach to divorce but manages to tackle the problem by its concept of annulment. Before I am accused of not understanding what an annulment is, I should explain that I devoted an entire chunk of a previous book to the subject, interviewed numerous priests and academics about it, and have studied how annulments are granted or refused in various diocese and particular countries. There is without doubt a certain form of cold logic behind the annulment process but it's not enormously Biblical. Adultery, for example, is not a reason for annulling a marriage nor, for that matter, is abuse or cruelty. The Catholic Church will annul a marriage if it can be proved that in the eyes of the Church the marriage never actually existed in the first place, was not valid in a Catholic sense, or was entered into without full disclosure or a commitment to the demands of the sacrament. Sometimes this policy is applied with a fair degree of compassion and even leniency, at other times far less so, and the inconsistency of these decisions is a bit of a running joke within Catholic circles. Frankly, that's up to the Catholic Church, but the point is that Catholicism has found a way to allow divorce, even if they're still saying "It's not a divorce, it's an annulment." It's a divorce.

Obviously I am not arguing from all this that divorce should be banned or that churches should become less tolerant of marriages that fall apart, but I am pointing out that the most apparently Biblical people can be the least Biblical people when it comes to issues that affect them directly and personally. Divorce rates are as high as 50 per cent in some countries and some churches, so imagine the result if Christian denominations suddenly rejected divorced people from their congregations. It's so much easier to be ostensibly "Biblical" to gay people, who constitute perhaps a mere 5 per cent of the population. It's a numbers game and a comfort game and a "not rocking the boat" game.

Nor has a rigid and anachronistic understanding of scripture always led to a positive and enlightened attitude toward women's equality. Regarding the struggle for female suffrage, of just giving women the vote, the Council of Congregational-ist Ministers of Massachusetts, basing its response on a literal interpretation of Genesis 1–2 and 1 Timothy 2 argued that "the appropriate duties and influence of woman are stated in the New Testament. . . . The power of woman is in her depend-ence, flowing from the consciousness of the weakness which God has given her for her protection. . . . When she assumes the place and tone of man as a public reformer . . . she yields the power which God has given her . . . and her character becomes unnatural." They were not alone, and as late as the early twen-tieth century many evangelical leaders in particular opposed women gaining the vote and also rejected a gender equality we would now take for granted. It's worth reflecting on that state-ment: what we now take for granted. Any church that publicly opposed a woman's right to vote would now be dismissed as perverse, unbalanced, hateful, and irrelevant yet a century ago that view was considered relatively mainstream and very often those Christians who disagreed were condemned as having lost or betrayed their Biblical faith. If that scenario sounds fam-iliar, it has been replicated several times in Christian history and is still alive and kicking.

Jeffrey John is an Anglican priest and dean of St. Albans in Britain. He has written delicately and convincingly about Christian approaches to homosexuality, both as a Christian man who is gay and as someone who was forced by conserva-tive pressure to step away from a bishopric that had been offered to him in 2003. The case was shameful, with an immensely and intensely qualified cleric fulfilling the demands of the Church of England – he is in a celibate, committed rela-tionship with another man – pressured out of the position by a loud, sometimes ugly, and often angry coalition of anti-gay

Christians both within and outside of his church. His calm, gracious, and quintessentially Christian reaction to the campaign was admirable. All of what he has written about this subject is worthy but let me quote just one brief section: "The scriptural arguments around gay relationships also run parallel to the scriptural arguments around the ordination of women. Both issues relate to creation ordinances, and especially to particular Pauline passages which seem to rule out both homosexual practice and female leadership on the basis of those ordinances. But of course everything depends on the hermeneutic you apply. A literal exegesis will no doubt rule out same-sex relationships, but it would equally rule out giving any authority to women (let alone ordaining them). Even more strongly, not just on the basis of Paul's teaching, but on the basis of Jesus' own teaching in four separate Gospel passages as well as in Paul, it would rule out the remarriage of divorcees as being equivalent to adultery. I suppose one might just about respect those who reject gay relationships on the basis of scripture, provided they also veil women, forbid them to speak in church, and condemn the remarried as adulterers."[5]

In some ways the most pertinent of all the past issues and examples is that of interracial marriage and Christian attitudes toward race in general. Under the apartheid system in South Africa right up until the early 1990s, some Christians and even entire churches based their defence of racial separation and segregation on scripture, and it wasn't long ago that full denominations in South Africa were proud of such teachings. The vast majority of those churches have since changed their minds and their understanding of Biblical instruction. In 1967 in the United States, a U.S. Supreme Court decision struck down laws in sixteen states that prohibited interracial marriage, but in 1959 the Virginia trial judge in a case that led directly to the 1967 decision made the following argument: "Almighty God created the races white, black, yellow, malay and red, and he placed them on separate continents. And but for the interference with his arrangement there would be no cause for such marriages. The fact that he separated the races shows that he did not intend for the races to mix." This was said in living memory – the year I was born, in fact – and such an attitude is far from extinct among certain Christian communities – there are still churches in the southern states of the United States that effectively disallow mixed-race couples. As recently as 2011, a major poll found that while 9 per cent of Americans opposed interracial marriage, 16 per cent of white evangelical Christians were against it; 27 per cent of Americans believed mixed marriages were beneficial while only 17 per cent of evangelicals thought so. Of course, we have to consider other factors such as class and education but those numbers are too consistent and too obvious to simply disregard.[6] It can't be denied, however, that most Christians today would be appalled at the idea that the Bible stood against people of different races enjoying a lifelong and loving commitment and receiving a church wedding or the sacrament of marriage. They reject those references of the Old Testament that forbid interracial marriages and believe them to apply exclusively to a specific period when the Jewish people were under unique pressures and threats or were given special commands by God that were only relevant thousands of years ago. How odd, then, that some of the very same people who readily embrace those sophisticated, realistic, compassionate, and sincere arguments about race cannot also apply them to contemporary issues of homosexuality.

So a certain pattern is emerging here, and it's not particularly difficult to perceive it. Christians have for generations and even centuries grappled to find ways to reinterpret scriptural references to divorce, and now try to forget the reality that not so long ago churches resisted demands for basic and self-evident justice by relying on the same Bible that is now used to resist equal marriage. In addition to divorce or racial and gender equality, we could list numerous subjects where a pedantic approach has and will land us in all sorts of trouble. The central problem occurs when we seem to have forgotten the quintessential message of Christ and instead hold on to less vital words to justify prejudice. We have to approach the Bible as a book written by many people over many centuries, with a specific purpose at a specific time, to be understood in its time and of its time. All of scripture is important but not all of it is supposed to be literal truth; its final, messianic figure and defining character is Jesus Christ. The conclusion of the story is His love, His forgiveness, His understanding, His compassion, His intimacy, His gentleness, and His utterly surprising and liberating reluctance to emulate the Pharisees and the legalists and obsess about sex and condemn those who do not fulfill the demands of a religious code in a specific era. Those who use the Bible as a document to condemn are transforming a living text into a dead volume and that, irony of ironies, is the most anti-Biblical act possible. I will be absolutely candid and probably offend people on all sides. I'm not really sure if the Bible openly and explicitly supports same-sex love and equal marriage but I think there's a good argument to say that it does and an even better argument to say that it doesn't really have an opinion on the subject that applies to the modern world. I am more convinced, however, that it doesn't condemn it and that we've got this one wrong for far too long.

I believe that just as we know so much more today about any number of scientific, physiological, and biological issues than we did a hundred, let alone two thousand years or five thousand years ago, we know far more about sexuality and in particular homosexuality than we did then. Remember, the term *homosexuality* was not even coined until the late nineteenth century and we knew hardly anything about it, seldom discussed it, and often criminalized it. There are very few people left in the Western world who would support the incarceration of gay people because of their sexuality or relationships but thousands of gay men were arrested and imprisoned as recently as the 1950s and 1960s; such appalling treatment was considered entirely acceptable by the majority of the population. So the idea that we have not changed in our understanding of the subject is absurd. The Bible teaches us a great deal about the nature of good and evil, about God's plan for salvation, and about the life of Jesus Christ but it was never intended as a guide for sexual and romantic conduct for people who would read it thousands of years later. I know that this will not convince the diehards, but for those who do still disagree, let's look at a few stories that might lead us to a different conclusion. In others word, before we move on to those surprisingly few passages of scripture that even discuss homosexuality, it's worth addressing some parts of the Bible from both testaments that might at least stimulate discussion. We'll begin with the story of David and Jonathan in the Old Testament.

There's a lot to discuss here in the famous story of the relationship between the son of King Saul and the man who would be king. David is a hero of scripture and a sculptor, killer of Goliath, founder of empire, distant relative of Jesus, and the man who certainly loved Jonathan. It's a relationship that has long been explained as the epitome of brotherly love and male bonding; even Oscar Wilde at his notorious trial claimed that his relationship with Lord Alfred Douglas, which was a gay romance, was akin to the story of David and Jonathan. As David is one of the key characters of scripture, the Christian, or for that matter Jewish, world could hardly argue that this was anything other than two noble warriors loving each other as bosom buddies. I remember as a very young boy at Hebrew classes on a Sunday morning wondering why we were hearing about two men who sounded like the sort of people we were otherwise told to fear and mock. If we're honest about it, some of the language in the story is certainly challenging. In 1 Samuel 18:1–4 we are told that "when David had finished speaking to Saul, the soul of Jonathan was bound to the soul of David, and Jonathan loved him as his own soul. Saul took him that day and would not let him return to his father's house. Then Jonathan made a covenant with David, because he loved him as his own soul. Jonathan stripped himself of the robe that he was wearing, and gave it to David, and his armor, and even his sword and his bow and his belt." Going back to the Hebrew school reference, I wasn't the only one in the class who giggled when the teacher read this to us in Hebrew as well as English but this was the 1960s and we were very quickly silenced and told to grow up. But surely it was precisely the grown-up part of us that led to the confusion and the embarrassment. I couldn't help thinking then, and far more so now, what we would conclude if Jonathan were Julie or Gillian – the story would seem much more understandable and "normal." For a man to give what were at that time his most prized possessions, including what he was wearing, to another man the first time they met was baffling to me.

Anybody who knows the story will recall how King Saul, gradually losing his control and probably his mind, turns his temper on David and argues with his son Jonathan over this young man. Jonathan is desperate and concerned and goes to find David in secret to warn him of his father's anger and hysteria. "David rose from beside the stone heap and prostrated himself with his face to the ground. He bowed three times and they kissed each other and wept with each other; David wept the more. Then Jonathan said to David, 'Go in peace, since both of us have sworn in the name of the Lord, saying, "The Lord shall be between me and you, and between my descendants and your descendants, forever."' He got up and left and then Jonathan went into the city" (1 Samuel 20:41–42). This was their final encounter, and after Jonathan was killed and David became king, he adopted his friend's son as his own, which was extraordinarily rare at the time. And then we have that beautiful, moving but oh so troubling passage in 2 Samuel 1:23, 26–27: "Saul and Jonathan, beloved and lovely! In life and in death they were not divided; they were swifter than eagles, they were stronger than lions. How the mighty have fallen in the midst of battle! Jonathan lies slain upon your high places. I am distressed for you my brother Jonathan; Greatly beloved were you to me; your love to me was wonderful, passing the love of women."

Try as we might, it's difficult not to be at least curious as to what this is all about. The author of the first and second books of Samuel was close to the royal court and knew the details of David's life, and if we're going to take other Biblical passages as literal truth, it's difficult to pass this one off as mere poetry and sexually ambivalent hyperbole. Has any genuinely and completely heterosexual man ever told another man that their love was more wonderful than that of a woman? This is more Sparta, Greece, than Sparta, Illinois. If that's too cryptic, the ancient Spartans accepted and even encouraged their warriors to form homosexual relationships, while in the Midwestern United States, not so much! Some of the Hebrew vocabulary used to describe the relationship between these two men is identical to that used to describe male-female relationships elsewhere in the Old Testament, and although there are no explicit references to same-sex romance, the story is extremely similar to that of Greek male warriors – see good old Sparta – who were obviously lovers. Remember, the book of Samuel was written centuries before we understood or acknowledged gay relationships in the way we do today. Once again, I am not claiming that the story of David and Jonathan is an example of two men who were gay lovers, but I am asking people to consider the story and ask honest questions about the example, the language, the attitude of the participants and the writer and to draw their own conclusions without prejudice. It's a beautiful and moving account and one with far more credibility and grace concerning this subject than those legal codes so often recited and quoted with the sole purpose of condemning gay people. And if my teacher at Hebrew school is still alive and reading this right now, you were lovely and are in no way responsible for this book.

Fast forward to the New Testament and the books of both Matthew and Luke. As I've already mentioned more than once, Jesus doesn't refer specifically to homosexuality and thus certainly doesn't condemn it. But, the argument goes, just because He doesn't actually mention it doesn't mean He didn't think of it as a sin and certainly doesn't imply that He approved of it. After all, the argument continues, the Old Testament does condemn homosexuality and Jesus said He came to complete the law and not break it. The problem with that line of thinking is that, as we will see shortly, the Old Testament is far more ambiguous than some would have us believe and, anyway, Jesus in fact did reform the ancient laws and tried to cut through the forest of legalism to show His followers the love and justice that was at the centre of God's teaching. He certainly took the trouble to expose all sorts of sins and expose religious hypocrisy but didn't list same-sex attraction as one of them. Nor will it do to argue that homosexuality simply wasn't an issue in the Roman-occupied Jewish world of the time because we know that it most certainly was and that Jesus's followers and listeners would have been well aware of it. As for Christ not having had to be specific and not, for example, condemning terrorism or abuse or rape, this line of reasoning just won't fly. He might not have mentioned terrorism or rape but He did refer to violence, injustice, and lust. There's also a bit of a contradiction here. Opponents of equal marriage make the case that Jesus's silence on homosexuality either means that it was so obvious to Him that it was wrong that it wasn't worth mentioning or that it was so little-known that it never occurred to Him to discuss it. Mind you, while Jesus didn't speak of the issue, some of His more conservative followers have certainly made up for the omission two thousand years later!

But back to Matthew and John. One of the best known and loved parts of the story of Jesus, and one that might actually show the contrary to what we've assumed, concerns a relationship that is deeply moving even at first glance. At second look, however, Jesus may well have been speaking of what He knew to be a loving gay relationship. Matthew 8:5–13 has it thus:

When Jesus had entered Capernaum, a centurion came to him, asking for help. "Lord," he said, "my servant lies at home paralyzed, suffering terribly."

Jesus said to him, "Shall I come and heal him?"

The centurion replied, "Lord, I do not deserve to have you come under my roof. But just say the word, and my servant will be healed. For I myself am a man under authority, with soldiers under me. I tell this one, 'Go,' and he goes; and that one, 'Come,' and he comes. I say to my servant, 'Do this,' and he does it."

When Jesus heard this, he was amazed and said to those following him, "Truly I tell you, I have not found anyone in Israel with such great faith. I say to you that many will come from the east and the west, and will take their places at the feast with Abraham, Isaac and Jacob in the kingdom of heaven. But the subjects of the kingdom will be thrown outside, into the darkness, where there will be weeping and gnashing of teeth."

Then Jesus said to the centurion, "Go! Let it be done just as you believed it would." And his servant was healed at that moment.

It's a delightful, startling account of a faith so strong that it leads to a miracle, and a faith so strong from someone who is not Jewish but a Roman and a Roman soldier, a hated occupier, at that. What we're seeing here is the faith of the Gentiles at work and how Jesus is willing to shower His love and power on all people and not just the Jews. Anybody who trusts so deeply will be rewarded. It's important to realize how hated the Romans were by most of the Jewish people and in particular by the powerless and the poor, those with whom Jesus spent so much of His time. The Jewish leadership and monarchy had originally turned to the emerging power of Rome as an ally, but by the time of Jesus the Romans were heartily detested, and within a few years a long and violent military uprising took place, leading to the deaths of many Roman soldiers and even more Jews. A people without the means to resist will express their contempt in whatever way they can, and one of the regular taunts thrown at the Romans by the Jews was that they participated in homosexual affairs; not only was the accusation generally believed but it was often true as well. It would have been no surprise at all to those listening to this story that the centurion in question had taken this slave as a lover and it may have even been assumed that this was the case. Shocking, surprising, just a modern, liberal ploy to try to justify an acceptance of gay people and equal marriage and base it on a beloved Jesus story? Actually, it's not as easy as that to dismiss this story, and there may be much more involved in it than what you've just read. In the Greek original of this Gospel, the word used by Matthew to describe the servant of the Roman soldier is *pais*, which in the first century had three different definitions: it could describe a son or mean *boy*; it could describe a servant; or it could be a specific reference to a servant who was a gay lover, often a younger man or even a teenager.[7] When Luke recounts the same story, he uses various Greek words that have other connotations. He describes the centurion's slave as an *entimos doulos* and although *doulos* was a generic word used to describe a slave, it was not used to denote a son or a boy so, in other words, the man in question could not have been the Roman soldier's son. But *entimos* is best trans-lated as *honoured* so we now have someone who was not a son, not an ordinary slave, but someone who while a servant was particularly special and loved by the centurion.[8] Interesting. The Bible contains other examples of people being healed but the request for the healing comes from family members or from close, intimate, loved people; in this case, it is a hardened soldier, the backbone of the Roman military machine, pleading that his beloved friend – his slave – should be restored to health.

We have to understand the story in context. Yes, there's that word again. Slaves were regarded as property, to be used or abused at will. If they died, so be it. Exceptions might arise if a slave was female and the slave's owner had formed a sexual union with her that became something greater and romantic or if the slave was male and after many years of service had become an advisor or an intellectual companion to an owner or a father figure to the children of the family. None of those examples explains this incident, and if we combine these circumstances with the popular understanding of Roman soldiers and their sexual use of both male and female slaves, a certain picture emerges that certainly causes us to rethink what we are reading. Once again, it would be sweeping and even unfair to offer this as conclusive and absolute proof of Jesus's acceptance of gay relationships, and I don't here do so, but my goodness, it challenges and dents the established point of view.

Beyond the Gospels, the Acts of the Apostles also offer an anecdote that merits deeper discussion. In chapter 8:26–40 we're told this story:

Now an angel of the Lord said to Philip the Evangelist, "Rise and go toward the south to the road that goes down from Jerusalem to Gaza." This is a desert place. And he rose and went. And there was an Ethiopian, a eunuch, a court official of Candace, queen of the Ethiopians, who was in charge of all her treasure. He had come to Jerusalem to worship and was returning, seated in his chariot, and he was reading the prophet Isaiah. And the Spirit said to Philip, "Go over and join this chariot." So Philip ran to him and heard him read-ing Isaiah the prophet and asked, "Do you understand what you are reading?" And he said, "How can I, unless someone guides me?" And he invited Philip to come up and sit with him. Now the passage of the Scripture that he was reading was this: "Like a sheep he was led to the slaughter and like a lamb before its shearer is silent, so he opens not his mouth. In his humiliation justice was denied him. Who can describe his generation? For his life is taken away from the earth." And the eunuch said to Philip, "About whom, I ask you, does the prophet say this, about himself or about someone else?" Then Philip opened his mouth, and beginning with this Scripture he told him the good news about Jesus. And as they were going along the road they came to some water, and the eunuch said, "See, here is water! What prevents me from being baptized?" And he commanded the chariot to stop, and they both went down into the water, Philip and the eunuch, and he baptized him. And when they came up out of the water, the Spirit of the Lord carried Philip away, and the eunuch saw him no more, and went on his way rejoicing. But Philip found himself at Azotus, and as he passed through he preached the gospel to all the towns until he came to Caesarea.

The Greek word used in Acts of the Apostles is *eunouchos* or *guardian* or *keeper* of the couch and was used only when describing men who were completely trusted by monarchs, royal families, and rulers. The eunouchos would be employed to care for and guard women, often high-ranking women, in similarly high-ranking families and thus had to be beyond risk.[9] They often became powerful and important themselves and in this case the eunuch in question was treasurer to the Queen of Ethiopia. As the word indicates, some of these men were literally castrated but we now know with our modern understanding of science and physiology that castration does not necessarily expunge all sexual desire and can even make men more sexually and physically aggressive. Those who lived two thousand years ago may not have understood the intricacies of where and how testosterone is made in the male body but they would have surely known by tradition and experience that physical castration was not always effective. It prevented procreation but not necessarily the desire to have sex. It's all rather complicated and certainly sad but this is where the concept of what were known as "natural" or "born" eunuchs comes into play, and there are numerous references in ancient culture to men who had no sexual or romantic attraction to women and were thus classified as eunuchs even though they were physically intact. We obviously have no idea whether the man mentioned in the book of Acts was a physical eunuch and we also do not know that he would have been associated with a group of men who were regarded as having links to homosexuality. As far back as Deuteronomy 23:1, the Bible stated, "No one whose testicles are crushed or whose penis is cut off shall be admitted to the assembly of the Lord," and by the time of Jesus and the early church this sorry and unfortunate – and unlucky – category included even those who could not have children; indeed, first-century Judaism refused conversion to such men. But here we have Philip refusing to judge or condemn this man and instead inviting him into the church and into a relationship with Jesus Christ. He didn't ask the eunuch to change his nature if he was gay, he didn't read him passages from an ancient text, and he didn't inquire whether he was a literal eunuch or someone defined as such because he was homosexual – he merely loved him unconditionally.

It's this overwhelming quality of unconditional love that so characterizes the ministry of Jesus yet He combines it with an unprecedented understanding of human nature. As described earlier, Christ is radical in His criticisms of divorce partly because of the sheer injustice involved and the pain, poverty, and disgrace it caused to women, and this led to some of His followers – mostly men – questioning the strictness of the teaching. It also led to further speculation that applies in this discussion. If divorce is so wrong, some of His people responded, maybe it would be better not to marry at all. Jesus responds in Matthew 19:11–12, "Not everyone can accept this teaching, but only those to whom it is given. For there are eunuchs who have been so from birth, and there are eunuchs who have been made eunuchs by others, and there are eunuchs who have made themselves eunuchs for the sake of the kingdom of heaven. Let anyone accept this who can."

So here we have Jesus listing three types of men who should not marry: those who have been made eunuchs by others and we must assume have been physically castrated; those who have opted to be eunuchs and, we assume, have chosen celibacy so as to devote their lives entirely to the service of God; and a third group consisting of men who were born eunuchs. If the latter is meant to be men who were born without testicles, we are entering the realm of absurdity – such events are so incredibly rare as to be irrelevant and would never have been included in such a profound statement about the nature of marriage, faith, and God. More than this, other such references in ancient texts to those born as eunuchs never refer to boys born with deformities but something entirely different.[10] So is Jesus speaking in entirely neutral and non-judgemental terms of gay men, of men born gay and "baby, they were born that way"? Many modern theologians, by no means all of them gay or even especially progressive, believe exactly this and they write from Catholic as well as Protestant perspectives.

So far these references have been to men and male homo-sexuality. Time for some equal gender time and back to the Old Testament – consider the story of Ruth and Naomi. It's often said that women have a limited profile in the Bible, and to an extent this is doubtless true but remember that Mary is the Mother of God, treated with such enormous respect by Catholics – Roman as well as Anglican – and was similarly respected by most of the great Protestant reformers, if not their successors. The first people to see the resurrected Jesus were women, not always believed by their male comrades, and two entire books of the Bible – Esther and Ruth – are named after women. The latter begins with the tale of Naomi and her husband, Elimelech, who are from Bethlehem – literally City of Bread, one of the most significant towns in scripture as it's literally and metaphorically important in the life of Jesus. In Naomi's case, a major famine forces her and her family to flee to Moab, which is part of another nation and of a different culture. Here Naomi's husband dies, and many years later her sons marry two women named Ruth and Orpah. But tragedy strikes again and both sons die, leaving the three women alone and isolated. That isolation meant something entirely different in the society of the time, in which women were generally either daughters or wives and were natural victims to the men and circumstances around them if they didn't have any male support. There are various precedents in Biblical texts such as

First and Second Kings and Genesis 38 where we see how vulnerable widows in particular were, so it's no surprise that Naomi decides to return to Bethlehem even though the city is still troubled. She also tells her daughters-in-law to in turn return to their own homes.[11] Orpah does so but Ruth cannot. She explains that she is too close to Naomi to leave her and we are told that she "clung" to Naomi. The word in Hebrew used to describe how she felt and how she acted is *dabaq*, which is the same word used in Genesis to describe Adam's attachment to Eve. Ruth says, "Do not press me to leave you or to turn back from following you! Where you go, I will go; where you lodge I will lodge; your people shall be my people, and your God my God. Where you die, I will die – there will I be buried. May the Lord do thus and so to me, and more as well, if even death parts me from you!"

Powerful, beautiful, and moving sentiments and often used even today when speaking of or conducting a marriage. If we combine these with the meaning of that word *dabaq*, we have a little explaining to do. When the word is used in the context of Adam and Eve, it refers to a man leaving his parents, growing up, and "clinging" to his wife. That can't simply be dismissed as coincidence – language is specific and used with a purpose. Scripture then tells us of Ruth and Naomi's life together and how they were devoted to and sacrificed for one another. Ruth does marry in the end but to a man much older than she and in a union based not on love – romance is never mentioned – but on the need to find someone to help Ruth and Naomi survive financially. Eventually Ruth has a baby boy from her marriage of convenience but it's interesting how the father of the child is not mentioned, but we are, on the other hand, told of Naomi's delight at the news. The local women state, "A son has been born to Naomi" (Ruth 4:17) and tell her that Ruth "who loves you, is more to you than seven sons" (Ruth 4:15).

Again, just as I said earlier, I am not convinced that this story is about a same-sex couple, and I would never demand for a moment that Christians have to understand it as such. It is foremost about devotion and love, it could be about mixed-race romance, it could be about the nature of conversion and the definition of who and what is a follower of God or who is Jewish, it could be about tolerance and the non-racial nature of God's plan. But it could also be about something else entirely. Just as with those few passages trotted out so repeatedly in their uniform ranks to condemn homosexuals and homosexuality, this part of scripture could also be about something else entirely if we think about it.

Which brings us to those regiments of text that are supposed to close the argument once and for all. Less regiments really, more tiny raiding parties. These are the difficult bits, the challenging quotes or what have been labelled the "clobber" passages of scripture. There are very few of them and most require, nay demand, a new, informed, and enlightened interpretation. The British evangelical leader Steve Chalke describes these half-dozen verses as "the six bullets in the gun." Alas, he is right and they have been used as ammunition far too often and with dark and painful results. Some people who use them shoot to kill. Chalke, by the way, is one of the victims of the firing squad. He's a highly respected Christian leader who became a popular and accepted spokesman for the Christian world through his work on television and on behalf of the homeless. There were few more effective Christian voices in the entire country. He remains an orthodox Christian but in 2014 made public his change of heart over equal marriage and gay rights. As a straight man and a follower of Christ, he announced he had, after much prayer and reflection, changed his position. He was immediately condemned by many and expelled from various Christian bodies and groups, as I will discuss later in greater detail. It's a tragically unfair but familiar scenario.

In 1962 the film production companies Pathé, sgc, and Titanus co-produced a movie called *Sodom and Gomorrah*, known in the United States as *The Last Days of Sodom and Gomorrah*. Bible epics were popular at the time, and with the dashing Stewart Granger, a sexy co-star, and an impressive cast, great things were expected. As it turned out, it was a truly awful movie, and the line that perhaps best sums up the ineptitude and unintentional humour of the thing came very early with the cry "Watch out for Sodomite patrols!" Watch out indeed. The movie came and went but Sodom is still discussed and quoted to a degree that is breathtaking when we consider its meagre historical and theological importance. Sodom has a great deal for which to answer. As for Gomorrah, we hardly knew you. Silly movies aside, the hurt and damage caused by a callow and rash interpretation of this relatively trivial and often totally misunderstood slice of Old Testament story is virtually beyond measure. I often think that Heaven must weep at the brokenness, devastation, suicide, family breakdown, and sheer terror provoked and produced by a few words written so long ago, and at how eager so many of Christ's followers are to use this story not to better appreciate God, but to better exclude some of His creatures.

The centre of the story is contained in Genesis 19:4–6. "Before they lay down, the men of the city, the men of Sodom, surrounded the house, both young and old, all the people from every quarter; and they called to Lot and said to him, 'Where are the men who came to you tonight? Bring them out to us that we may have relations with them.' But Lot went out to them at the doorway, and shut the door behind him." Good old Lot. But let's take a closer look at what was actually going on here.

Abraham, formerly known as Abram, one of the central figures not only of the Christian but also the Jewish and Muslim faiths, has a nephew called Lot who went to live in Sodom, which was then regarded as one of the more modern and advanced cities of the ancient Middle East but also considered a place of great evil. For Lot it was an alternative to the desert, rural life of his uncle, who lived an essentially nomadic exist- ence. But along with all that modernity, wealth, and comfort went wickedness; the city of Sodom was decadent and popu- lated by immoral people, although we're not told exactly what sort of evil they got up to but are given broad brushstrokes of the nasty picture. Because of the city's reputation for evil, God tells Abraham that Sodom is to be destroyed as an example to others and indeed two angels are sent to Sodom to find out if the stories of evil are true; they visit Abraham's nephew to stay, to be fed, and to be looked after and so on. Lot doesn't realize his visitors are angels but he knows that strangers must be pro- tected and treated kindly, both because this is the holy and righteous way to live and also because he himself had been in such a position not so long ago. All proceeds well but in the evening the people from the city come to Lot's door having learned that he has welcomed two strangers and they demand that Lot send his guests out to them so that they might "know them" – the Hebrew word used in Genesis is sometimes, though not always, used to denote sex or sexual intercourse, and while some scholars doubt that meaning in this context we can prob- ably accept it in this case as meaning sex. Lot is outraged and argues with those outside his door, explaining that what they want is wrong and evil. As an alternative he suggests that he send his virgin daughters out to them instead but the people outside the door insist on those apparently irresistible strangers and try to smash their way inside the house. As a consequence, the angels cause those shouting and threatening to become blind and then explain to Lot that he and his family have to leave Sodom because God will indeed destroy the place. The following day, a great fire is sent from heaven and Sodom is wiped out and its population killed.

The story is not new to most of us, and for centuries it's been the foundational episode for the Christian assumption that homosexuality is evil and immoral and as a consequence has led to the marginalization, condemnation, and even persecution and slaughter of gay people. But it doesn't require a theologian or an ancient historian to realize that there are some gigantic inconsistencies about the story and some worrying implications. First of all, it's not in any way certain that this text was always considered to apply to homosexuality and may well have been given that connotation for the first time by Jewish scribes living between the era of the Old and New Testaments who wanted to further differentiate Jews from Gentiles. Knowing that several non-Jewish cultures of the time accepted homosexuality, they attempted to define homosexuality as one of the key characteristics of Gentile morality and insisted that it had been condemned by God in Genesis to the point of the total destruction of a city and people. So understanding the chronology of all this matters very much indeed if we are to respect the Bible in the way it so richly deserves.

Beyond how the very meaning may have been changed centuries after the text was written, today the terms *sodomy* and *sodomites*, while archaic and offensive to most in the West, thank goodness, are still used to describe homosexuality and homosexuals and in my experience are coming back into use among the religious right as they become militant in the face of increasing isolation and defeat. For many centuries, the terms have certainly been used, all leading back to an obscure event that occurred thousands of years ago in a place we can't directly identify any longer but is somewhere in the Middle Eastern desert. The words in the story are vitally important and we have to get them right if we're to appreciate the meaning and purpose of all this. The Bible says that "the men of Sodom, both young and old, all the people to the last man" come to Lot's house, to his door, and shout that his guests must be brought to them. Not just some of the people in the city, not just those who were known to be homosexual, not just the adults, but all of them. Now even the most committed conspiracy theorist or paranoid homophobe would have a problem with those sorts of numbers! Seriously though, while we'll never know exactly how many people in any society have same-sex attractions, the highest estimate has been 10 per cent and the more usual estimation is closer to 5 per cent. In Sodom and its sister city, however, we are led to believe that everybody was homo-sexual. Quite clearly this is absurd. Also, remember that Lot offers his virgin daughters to the hysterical mob in place of the two male strangers, which would indicate that the would-be rapists outside the door desire not men as such but any person they can gang-rape and abuse. It's also necessary to say that the people who use this part of scripture to condemn homo-sexuality and advocate what they claim to be "family values" might have some trouble justifying a father offering to sacri-fice his virgin daughters as mass rape victims in an effort to preserve two people who have just visited. I've yet to read any such family advice in the many evangelical and Catholic magazines that I've looked at over the years.

This is surely an account not of homosexuality but of the evils of animalistic sex, rape, abuse, and the treatment of other people as sexual objects. In ancient cultures and even in the modern world to a deeply troubling extent, rape of captured men, and of course women, by conquering soldiers is an expression less of lust and sexuality than of dominance and sadism. Rape was and is still a weapon. In Judges 19 there is another and lesser known reference to gang rape where a mob surrounds the house: "Pounding on the door, they shouted to the old man who owned the house, 'Bring out the man who came to your house so we can have sex with him.' The owner of the house went outside and said to them, 'No, my friends, don't be so vile. Since this man is my guest, don't do this outrageous thing. Look, here is my virgin daughter, and his concubine. I will bring them out to you now, and you can use them and do to them whatever you wish. But as for this man, don't do such an outrageous thing.' But the men would not listen to him. So the man took his concubine and sent her outside to them, and they raped her and abused her throughout the night, and at dawn they let her go." Frankly, it's a little difficult to draw too many conclusions from all this and quite dangerous to even try to do so without a great deal of qualification and questioning. Yet the story of Sodom is used times beyond counting to explain not ancient crimes and punishment but to justify modern discrimination and, in some parts of Africa and the Caribbean in particular, assaults and even murder.

What we also have to realize is that even within the Bible itself there are references to the story of Sodom that contradict the standard understanding that it is a warning of the terrible consequences of homosexuality. Of the roughly twenty mentions of Sodom in scripture, none of them speaks of homosexuals. In Ezekiel, for example, we are told, "This was the guilt of your sister Sodom: She and her daughters had pride, excess of food, and prosperous ease, but did not aid the poor and needy. They were haughty and did abominable things before me; therefore I removed them when I saw it." So rather than condemning homosexuality, the book of Ezekiel is using the Sodom story to expose the sins of pride, gluttony, complacency and sloth, indifference to the poor, arrogance, and excess wealth. Isaiah speaks of Sodom as an example of lack of and abuse of justice; Jeremiah speaks of it in terms of general immorality; in the Book of Wisdom we are reminded that the men of Sodom refused to accept the strangers who visited their city; and Ecclesiasticus 16 says that the sin of Sodom was not homosexuality but pride. In the New Testament, Jesus speaks about those cities that refuse to greet and welcome His disciples and warns that their fate will be worse than that of Sodom. Not, remember, because of any sexual crime that has been committed there but because they have shown a lack of hospitality and have refused to embrace strangers, in this case strangers who follow the Messiah.

The Epistle of Jude 1:7 is sometimes used to support the homosexual aspect of the sin of Sodom but that's far from certain. In the King James translation of the Bible, we're given a slightly different interpretation of this. It says, "Even as Sodom and Gomorrha, and the cities about them in like manner, giving themselves over to fornication, and going after strange flesh, are set forth for an example, suffering the vengeance of eternal fire." Some versions have this as "sexual perversion" rather than "strange flesh" but no translation explicitly refers to homosexuality. The early seventeenth-century King James version is significant because "strange flesh" may well refer to the flesh of the "strangers" whom the mob wanted to rape and the repeated Biblical command to care for the well-being and safety of strangers. Or it could be a reference to those people – women as well as men – who wanted to have sex with angels rather than with humans and thus strange flesh. Even the more modern references to "sexual perversion" and "fornication" are in no way specific to same-sex activity and far more likely to indicate general promiscuity, abuse, loveless sex, and rape. It bears mentioning that the King James translation of the Bible is named after the monarch who commissioned it, and while happily married to his queen he also very much enjoyed the company of his handsome young male friends.

It may come as a surprise but it in fact took a long time for the story of Sodom to be directly associated with homosexuality, and it wasn't until several hundred years later, in the first century, that Jewish and Christian writers wrote of the link. Even then, however, they were far from unanimous. This occurred only in early medieval Europe, largely after Peter Damian – a cardinal who was later made a Doctor of the Church – wrote *The Book of Gomorrah* for Pope Leo ix around the year 1049. "Truly, this vice is never to be compared with any other vice because it surpasses the enormity of all vices. . . . It defiles everything, stains everything, pollutes everything. And as for itself, it permits nothing pure, nothing clean, nothing other than filth. . . . The miserable flesh burns with the heat of lust; the cold mind trembles with the rancor of suspicion; and in the heart of the miserable man chaos boils like Tartarus (Hell). . . . In fact, after this most poisonous serpent once sinks its fangs into the unhappy soul, sense is snatched away, memory is borne off, the sharpness of the mind is obscured. It becomes unmindful of God and even forgetful of itself. This plague undermines the foundation of faith, weakens the strength of hope, destroys the bond of charity; it takes away justice, subverts fortitude, banishes temperance, blunts the keenness of prudence. And what more should I say since it expels the whole host of the virtues from the chamber of the human heart and introduces every barbarous vice as if the bolts of the doors were pulled out."

And with that the accusation of sodomy and the persecution of those labelled as sodomites began its dark, bloody stain, one that continues to this day. James Kugel, who has served as both Starr Professor Emeritus of Classical and Modern Hebrew Literature at Harvard and chair of the Institute for the History of the Jewish Bible at Bar Ilan University in Tel Aviv, has written that early interpreters were "perplexed about the city of Sodom. God destroyed it because of the terrible things that were being done there – but what exactly were those things? Strangely, the Genesis narrative does not say." Richard Elliott Friedman, professor of Hebrew and Comparative Literature at the University of California, San Diego, has other questions. He writes, "The text says that two *people* come to Sodom, and that *all* of the *people* of Sodom come and say, 'Let's know them.' The homosexuality interpretation apparently comes from misunderstanding the Hebrew word *'anasim'* to mean 'men,' instead of people."[12] The truth is that there are valid debates to be had over ancient Hebrew, word structure, and intended meaning. So to every person who throws around references to Sodom, I strongly recommend a reading course, a great deal of thought, even more prayer, and perhaps more time reflecting on the love of Jesus than the activities of a rabid rape mob in the middle of an ancient desert.

Would that it ended there. Those Christians who oppose the demands of the gay community argue that if Genesis is a little ambiguous and Sodom not sufficiently convincing, we have what it says in Leviticus. But what does it actually say in the third book of the Bible? There are in fact two references in Leviticus to homosexuality; 18:22 has "Thou shalt not lie with mankind as with womankind; it is an abomination" or in the more modern New International Version (NIV), "Do not have sexual relations with a man as one does with a woman; that is detestable." Leviticus 20:13 has "If a man also lie with mankind as he lieth with a woman, both of them have committed an abomination; they shall surely be put to death; their blood be upon them" or, again in the NIV, "If a man has sexual relations with a man as one does with a woman, both of them have done what is detestable. They are to be put to death; their blood will be on their own heads." Appears pretty clear, whether in the older or in the more contemporary versions.

Some historical background before we continue. The writing of Leviticus probably dates back to the Jewish exile in Babylon and was written to encourage childbirth and an increased Jewish population during a time of enormous pressure on the Jews to convert, intermarry, and assimilate. There was a genuine danger of the Jewish people disappearing in their diaspora, and if they ever were to resettle in Israel they had to have the numbers to do so. This particular part of Leviticus was likely written by someone we know of as "The Priestly Writer" and was probably the same person who gave us in Genesis the creation story and the command to "go forth and multiply." Its commands were also a way to distinguish Jewish from Babylonian culture and society at a time when Babylon seemed increasingly tempting and welcoming to the Jews – enormous numbers of exiled Jewish people gradually came not only to accept but to embrace those who had conquered them. Ancient Babylon was not only tolerant of homosexuality but may well have included it in local forms of worship, and although Jews were not expected to participate they would be required to agree. It's important to avoid modern notions of conquering nations always treating the conquered with cruelty or persecuting them or even going so far as to institute some sort of genocide. They could be sadistic and murderous, but not always, and usually acted out of self-interest rather than ideology. Entire cultures disappeared in the ancient world not because of violence but because the dominant culture seemed to have more advantages than their own. Jews abandoned their faith both at this point and later, under especially Greek and even Roman rule, because they wanted to do so rather than had to do so. In Leviticus, we have Jewish religious leaders affirming that Jews and Gentiles were radically different and that part of that difference was the Gentile acceptance of homosexuality. To be Jewish meant to be straight. It was about establishing the ancient Jewish people as being special to the Lord and being different from others. Thing is, as we saw earlier in the letter written to Dr. Laura that is based firmly on authentic Biblical commands, being separate and special also requires a man's beard to be of a certain length, forbids the eating of shellfish, and lays down numerous other laws and rules written many thousands of years ago that most Jewish people now would consider absurd and, anyway, at no time had any application to Christians. Yes, I know that many Jews abstain from pork and shellfish: they might keep kosher to a lesser or greater extent but the vast majority of Jews wouldn't dream of observing every Mosaic law of demand written in Leviticus. As for Christians, to assume that all these Old Testament laws apply to a church is to be anti-Biblical and to disregard the conclusions of the early Christians that are made so abundantly clear in the New Testament. Christians do not need to be circumcised, do not need to keep kosher, and do not need to be Jewish.

But let's also take a look at the translations of the words involved and what they actually mean. This, by the way, is important. Translation can lead us astray just as often as it can illuminate meaning. It's significant that people with a certain theological, political, and moral axe to grind tend to cherry-pick particular words from different versions of scripture. They often, for example, use modern translations such as the New International Version or New Jerusalem for most of what they quote but then revert to the King James version of 1612 when it comes to homosexuality so that they can throw in the word *abomination*. And what a lovely word it is. Ask yourselves how often you have used this word to describe gay relationships and then remember that modern translations use a different term entirely. Mind you, to be fair we must admit that most contemporary versions still condemn the action, but it's more often interpreted as "taboo" or "detestable" or something that is "abhorrent." I admit that there is no getting around that description but only if we are also prepared to not get around the condemnation of intermarriage, child sacrifice, witchcraft, marrying a divorced woman, cross-dressing, cross-breeding animals, planting fields with different types of grain, and sacrificing bruised and damaged animals to God. Child murder I can understand, and I'd be apoplectic if someone tried to turn me into a newt but marrying someone who is divorced or dressing up as Madonna for a Halloween party? Surely not. As for anybody trying to kill me because of my Jack Russell-Golden Labrador mix, well let them just try.

Yes, all these actions are condemned with exactly the same type of language and equal enthusiasm elsewhere in scripture and only a lunatic or someone with a particular dislike of Madonna or Halloween parties or my dog would become so incredibly cross about it all. Flippant? Not so. This is exactly how anachronistic and ridiculous the blind, blanket application of ancient legal codes is to the modern conscience and mind. It's just plain silly yet has caused so much pain to so many people for so very long.

The prohibition of homosexuality is also deeply woven into ancient attitudes toward gender, women, and masculinity. We are speaking here of a culture of several thousand years ago when there was a steel-like patriarchy and, in a literal sense, patriarchs; indeed, the original patriarchs. This was a male-dominated society in which masculine values and virtues were the model and the rule, and for any man to act as a woman or allow himself to be treated like a woman was, yes, an abomination. The Leviticus reference is not to same-sex partnerships as we know and understand them, and such an interpretation of the text would be horribly reductive in that it refers to penetration, to men being used by other men as substitutes or alternatives to women, and to men, in the understanding of the writers of Leviticus, abandoning the essence of what made them manly. Thus it describes what would be thought shameful, what happened to prisoners of war, what might occur between non-Jews and between those who did not know and love God. It is also specifically about men and, as with almost all Biblical references to the gay issue, does not include or even consider lesbianism. If we're to be exact about this, it excludes half of all gay people and then many if not most gay men because only a limited number of them engage in penetrative sex, something we will look at further later in the book.

And, as again with most Biblical discussions, it concerns heterosexual men behaving in a non-heterosexual manner rather than gay men acting as gay men. This is important. The Bible doesn't really say anything about gays, it says a few things about heterosexuals behaving badly.

Beyond what these laws in Leviticus and elsewhere forbid, we should also consider what they demand. In Deuteronomy, for example, the ancient Hebrews are told that a man must marry his brother's widow and give her an heir. In context, and considering the vulnerable place of women and in particular widows, we can understand the morality and logic behind this command but only in that context. Otherwise it is nonsensical, bizarre, horribly intrusive, and completely irrelevant to a modern society. Which is how intelligent and faithful people should understand all these regulations. If we pick and choose which ones we believe and observe and which ones we don't, we are placing our own prejudices not only above common sense and intelligent reading but also above God's plan for His creatures. The Old Testament has much to tell us about the history of the ancient Hebrew people and it sets the scene for the great miracle to come, for the completion of the story, the coming of Jesus Christ, the Son of God. It shows the Jewish people in a negative as well as positive light, it shows men and women following God and betraying God, living as they should and living as they certainly should not. With regard to marriage and sexual relationships, it not only tells us very little but also presents models and examples that are jarring and sometimes deeply disturbing. Polygamy is common and often the norm, and the use of concubines or mistresses – frequently in an achingly exploitative manner – is readily accepted. The challenge of Christians is not to rely on the Old Testament to form arguments against loving, same-sex relationships but to convince other people that the Old Testament no longer applies and explain how we now look to committed two-person marriage rather than to male-dominated clans where women are used as sex objects. So-called traditional marriage is to a large extent an oxymoron, and the concept of family values is a worrying flexible one if we base it on what was done, said, and written in a desert culture almost three thousand years ago.

Which brings us to relatively more recent times and the New Testament. Once again, however, there is just as little said in the New as in the Old about homosexuality and, as we have already established, Jesus Himself never even mentions the subject. I know this might sound repetitive but it's still generally assumed that Christ Himself pronounced on this issue, and as we have seen He doesn't, unless it is implicitly through His acceptance of a centurion's love for a male slave. Paul, however, does so in his Letter to the Romans, 24–27: "Therefore God gave them over in the sinful desires of their hearts to sexual impurity for the degrading of their bodies with one another. They exchanged the truth about God for a lie, and worshiped and served created things rather than the Creator – who is forever praised. Amen. Because of this, God gave them over to shameful lusts. Even their women exchanged natural sexual relations for unnatural ones. In the same way the men also abandoned natural relations with women and were inflamed with lust for one another. Men committed shameful acts with other men, and received in themselves the due penalty for their error." To understand this properly, however, we need to show what Paul wrote both directly before and directly after this oft-quoted paragraph. Leading up to this, Paul writes in 21–23, "For although they knew God, they neither glorified him as God nor gave thanks to him, but their thinking became futile and their foolish hearts were darkened. Although they claimed to be wise, they became fools and exchanged the glory of the immortal God for images made to look like a mortal human being and birds and animals and reptiles," and immediately afterwards in 28–32: "Furthermore, just as they did not think it worthwhile to retain the knowledge of God, so God gave them over to a depraved mind, so that they do what ought not to be done. They have become filled with every kind of wickedness, evil, greed and depravity. They are full of envy, murder, strife, deceit, and malice. They are gossips, slanderers, God-haters, insolent, arrogant, and boastful; they invent ways of doing evil; they disobey their parents; they have no understanding, no fidelity, no love, no mercy. Although they know God's righteous decree that those who do such things deserve death, they not only continue to do these very things but also approve of those who practice them."

So if we follow the order of all this and not just isolate the verses ostensibly about homosexuality that are usually offered, we see a strict chronology develop. Paul writes first about those who refuse to acknowledge and honour God, then about those people who begin to worship idols, next how they become far more interested in earthly than spiritual pursuits, then how they abandon their natural desires for sex with people of the same gender, and finally how they disrespect their parents and are proud, envious, malicious, and argumentative. What he is writing about, in fact, is how they come to reject and hate God. It's important to appreciate that this letter is written to a church composed of both Jewish believers in Christ and Gentiles who have abandoned various pagan religions and cults for Christianity. In the first part of the letter, Paul seems to be criticizing those

Gentiles who have not lived up to the faith, and in the second he addresses the failing of the Jewish believers. As with most parts of scripture, there is a deliberate intent and a specific purpose here. It's also worth noting that this is the only passage anywhere in scripture that refers to female as well as male homosexuality. But what is it primarily about? Paul is obviously angry and disappointed at those who have exchanged what is right for what is wrong; he packages various failings, errors, and sins together, all of them resulting in a falling away from the glory of the one, true God. He uses the words *nature* and *natural* and is, always, specific in his choice of language. Yet in 1 Corinthians Paul asks us, "Does not nature itself teach you that if a man wears long hair, it is degrading to him?" In other words, we have to understand what is being written in terms of contemporary attitudes and those attitudes include the specific fashions and conventions of the time. Paul's question about hair length would have seemed anachronistic and irrelevant even a few years later, let alone several centuries later. Beware of taste masquerading as morality. For example, military swagger among many of Napoleon's cavalry troopers was indicated by long, flowing hair; the same martial spirit a century later in the French army was shown by close, cropped haircuts. Perhaps Paul's talk of sexuality here is more than a mere expression of fad, and I am not comparing sexual intimacy with tonsorial preference, but to apply opaque Pauline comments to same-sex relationships for all eternity is intellectually vacuous. Paul is speaking here of idolatry and of putting selfish desires and lusts before the worship of God. It's about forgetting God and expunging Him from the human equation, and Paul writes that this failing is demonstrated by all sorts of behaviour, including straight men indulging in what is unnatural to their characters. To gay men and women following

Christ today who have no inclination to worship anything or any person other than God and who have only ever felt romance and attraction to those of the same gender, this condemnation simply does not apply and has no spiritual or ethical meaning at all. It should matter not a jot to the homosexual but, my goodness, it matters a great deal to the homophobe.

We can only attempt to understand what is going on concerning this so sensitive subject in these ancient texts if we accept what is surely self-evident and what applies not only to scripture but to the writings of the early Christians to the church fathers: namely that there was no appreciation at this time that homosexuality was not some choice made by otherwise heterosexual men but something people felt from the earliest stages of their lives and perhaps from birth. Not even "felt" but "were." It was not a lifestyle choice, not an opinion, not an exchange of one form of sexuality for another but something intrinsic to character and being and far greater and deeper than mere sex. Yet the notion of "exchanging" is precisely what Paul refers to in his Letter to the Romans. Neither he nor his contemporaries were writing of gay couples but of sexual exploitation, of pagan abuse, and of physical aggression and loveless sex. Professor John Boswell is more ambivalent on the issue than many other historians who have reinterpreted Paul but he still has it thus: "The persons Paul condemns are manifestly not homosexual: what he derogates are homosexual acts committed by apparently heterosexual persons. . . . It is not clear that Paul distinguished in his thoughts or writings between gay persons (in the sense of permanent sexual preference) and heterosexuals who simply engaged in periodic homosexual behavior. It is in fact unlikely that many Jews of his day recognized such a distinction, but it is quite apparent that – whether or not he was aware of their existence – Paul did not discuss gay persons but only homosexual acts committed by hetero-sexual persons."[13]

James Brownson's book *Bible, Gender, Sexuality: Reframing the Church's Debate on Same-Sex Relationships* is a remarkable work on many levels but what he says about Paul's Letter to the Romans is especially vital. He speaks of how Paul is not being generic in his words but is directly referring to the Roman emperors Gaius and the infamous Caligula and their inter-national and, in the latter case, lasting reputations for immoral-ity and indulgence. Paul's readers and listeners would have known exactly whom he was describing and condemning, and it may well be that it is the lifestyles of the Roman, pagan lead-ers rather than same-sex attraction that we're speaking of here. The following is a long quotation but it's a vital one:

First of all, Gaius is closely linked to the practice of idolatry. The Roman writer Suetonius reports how Gaius "set up a special temple to his own godhead, with priests and with victims of the choicest kind." Another Roman writer, Dio Cassius, comments negatively on how Gaius was the only emperor to claim to be divine and to be the recipient of worship during his own lifetime. Gaius also tried at one point to erect a statue of himself in the Temple in Jerusalem; he was dissuaded only by a delegation from Herod Agrippa. Hence the link between Gaius and idolatry would have been well-known indeed, particularly in Jewish circles. But Gaius also serves as Exhibit A for out-of-control lust. Suetonius reports how Gaius "lived in perpetual incest with all his sisters, and at a large banquet he placed each of them in turn below him, while his wife reclined above." He records gruesome examples of Gaius's arbitrary violence, vindictiveness, and cruelty. Later, Suetonius chronicles Gaius's sexual liaisons with the wives of dinner guests, raping them in an adjoining room and then returning to the banquet to comment on their performance. Various same-sex sexual encounters between Gaius and other men are similarly recounted. Finally, a military officer whom he had sexually humiliated joined a conspiracy to murder him, which they did less than four years into his reign. Suetonius records that Gaius was stabbed through the genitals when he was murdered. One wonders whether we can hear an echo of this gruesome story in Paul's comments in Romans 1:27: "Men committed shameless acts with men and received in their own person the due penalty for their error." Gaius Caligula graphically illustrates the reality of which Paul speaks in Romans 1: the movement from idolatry to insatiable lust to every form of depravity, and the violent murderous reprisal that such behavior engenders.[14]

As with some of the earlier discussions in this chapter, it would be unwise, even smug, to draw many absolutes. Paul's Letter to the Romans is quite clearly not an easy passage for those of us who support equal marriage and the full acceptance of openly gay people into the Church, but neither is it an obvious call to prohibition and that is what it has been used as for many centuries not by a few but by most leaders of organized Christianity. Former Archbishop of Canterbury Rowan Williams, one of the finest modern theologians, made this point back in 2007 when he spoke at the University of Toronto. He told his audience that the passage in Romans that appears to refer to homosexuality was, if anything, a warning to

Christians that they should not be self-righteous and that its primary point was most certainly not about homosexuality at all. He argued that Paul was telling the Church that whenever they condemned others they were condemning themselves and he believed that the Letter to the Romans does not favour any side of the Christian argument in the gay debate. Of course, someone in his position had to be extremely careful with an Anglican communion severely divided on the issue and with conservatives willing to leave the Church and form their own denominations not over, for example, Christ's divinity or the truth of the trinity but a particular interpretation of half a dozen fairly brief passages in the Bible. Many of those conservatives, by the way, have already left and formed other churches because of just this.

Other historians and theologians have argued that Romans is about all forms of non-procreative sex; that it's about pedophilia, polygamy, or incest or the use of slaves or dominant, sadistic sex. I think that this part of Romans is more likely making the case that rejecting God has important and tragic consequences, including losing one's moral and sexual foundations. It includes within those moral and sexual foundations heterosexuals indulging in homosexuality or, for that matter, homosexuals indulging in heterosexual relationships. Both would be a denial of who we are, how we were made, and what God's genuine plan for us really is.

And so to the last of the "clobber" verses, both again from Paul – 1 Corinthians 6:7–11: "The very fact that you have lawsuits among you means you have been completely defeated already. Why not rather be wronged? Why not rather be cheated? Instead, you yourselves cheat and do wrong, and you do this to your brothers and sisters. Or do you not know that wrongdoers will not inherit the kingdom of God? Do not be deceived: Neither the sexually immoral nor idolaters nor adulterers nor men who have sex with men nor thieves nor the greedy nor drunkards nor slanderers nor swindlers will inherit the kingdom of God. And that is what some of you were. But you were washed, you were sanctified, you were justified in the name of the Lord Jesus Christ and by the Spirit of our God." And 1 Timothy 1:8–11, "We know that the law is good if one uses it properly. We also know that the law is made not for the righteous but for lawbreakers and rebels, the ungodly and sinful, the unholy and irreligious, for those who kill their fathers or mothers, for murderers, for the sexually immoral, for those practicing homosexuality, for slave traders and liars and perjurers – and for whatever else is contrary to the sound doctrine that conforms to the gospel concerning the glory of the blessed God, which he entrusted to me." I have quoted the words of the specific references to homosexuality here for a purpose as we're usually directed only to 1 Corinthians 6:9 and 1 Timothy 1:10. It's extremely important that we see the apparent condemnations in their context and how they are packaged. First, though, we need to discuss translation and what words actually mean here.

Two Greek terms used by Paul have been subjected to tendentious, perhaps misleading, and certainly inadequate translation down the years. Those words are *malakoi* and *arsenokoites*. The first means *softies* and it's used elsewhere in scripture and in general Greek to refer to clothes as well as to men; this is especially significant as there are other Greek words that could have been used that apply only to men who are the passive partners in homosexual sex. Malakoi is used to describe all sorts of soft or even pleasant activity such as fine food, warm baths, or clothes that are comfortable rather than rough on the skin. Some gay men may be soft and some anti-gay men like to regard gay men as soft but the homosexual troops of the Hellenic armies who were renowned for their courage and toughness were hardly thought of as softies by their enemies and those whom they defeated, and throughout history we have seen gay men be as strong, fearless, and hard as their heterosexual comrades. The gay man as soft or weak is a sometimes fashionable stereotype but has no basis in truth and seems profoundly odd for Paul to use if he's referring only to homosexuals. As we saw earlier, Roman soldiers also had a reputation for having gay sex and they were hardly regarded by first-century Jews as being soft. Arsenokoites is an equally bewildering choice as it's a contrived word actually conceived by Paul and had no earlier reference in Biblical or non-Biblical Greek. Its literal translation is *male-bedder* or a man who is willing to take the place of a woman in bed or become the passive partner in gay sex. But there's also a deeper meaning here because the word, the person, is listed along with those who exploit people financially or take economic advantage of others. In that case, we're probably better off thinking of male-bedders as male prostitutes or rent-boys, younger men selling themselves to older men – often heterosexual men – for money and gain. When the word is used again after its initiation by Paul, it is invariably listed as an economic sin or crime.[15] Both Clement of Alexandria and John Chrysostom discuss homosexuality in their writings but neither used the word *arsenokoitai* other than when they are quoting the very lists Paul uses in 1 Corinthians. If we're to construe anything from this, it's that Paul was not speaking of homosexuality. We have to ask why such a literate man, so well-versed in various languages and so in control of his vocabulary and meaning, would invent a word that would not be familiar to his readers rather than use words for homosexual that were far better known. More than this, when the word is used in future writings, in the example of Aristides in his Apology in the second century, it's to list the sins of the Greek gods and, in this case, likely to describe Zeus raping a young boy named Ganymede.

Beyond the translation is the nature and content of the list of activities Paul gives us that will apparently close the door to the kingdom of God. They include slander, perjury, drunkenness, greed, and lying, none of them to be admired, but more than a few critics of the gay community have been a little greedy, have drunk too much, and even told the odd lie. None of them, surely, would agree that this would close shut the doors of paradise. I can tell you from personal experience that some of the fiercest critics of equal marriage and homosexuality have lied about me on numerous occasions, as I made clear in my first chapter. Most balanced and worldly people with a sense of Christian empathy and compassion might still provide an occasional example of greed or a drunken evening. In other words, these are not very serious offences. What is indeed a serious offence is being a slave trader, which is also listed here. Yet as we saw earlier in this chapter, not only were slavers defended and justified by Christians for several centuries but their number included devout Christians and even ordained Christian ministers. The contradiction screams out, in whatever language we choose.

Entire books have been written about this Biblical debate and more will be written in the future.[16] Some have taken a more conservative position but the trend is generally for scholars to present a more liberal, revised, or progressive stance.

The more we learn about the nature of the first century and about the language, religion, and culture of the time, the more we question long-held opinions about what the Bible actually teaches on some of these difficult issues. All we know and understand of the Bible, all we read from it that influences and shapes our life, must be seen and felt through the filter of Jesus Christ. Christ-drenched scripture must inform and not infect our lives, and the absolute of love is not just *something* but *everything* to the Christian. If I were convinced that God condemned homosexuality, I would, no matter how painful, have to either embrace that fact or abandon my faith. It happens that I do not. The tragedy is that so many people, both gay and straight, have been led to believe that God certainly does reject gay people if they want to live a full and complete life, and many of them have, as a direct consequence, understandably left Christianity far behind. But I am now convinced that this is just not the case, that it never was, and that even if there was an ambiguity thousands of years ago, it was a direct application to a period and to a specific people and not to all time and to future generations. If I had any hair left, I would wear it as I liked and know God loved me. I will mix the cloths of my clothes and know that God loves me. I eat pork and bacon and even mix milk and meat and know that God loves me. But, in all honesty, I seldom eat shellfish – not that it would stop God loving me but I just don't like shellfish very much. I'm also straight. Not because being gay would stop God loving me and my partner and our marriage, but because I'm simply not gay. If I were gay, though, it would make being a Christian so much more difficult; and God wouldn't love that at all.

Let me conclude this chapter with a quotation from Dr. Daniel A. Helminiak, author of the seminal work *What the*

*Bible Really Says About Homosexuality.* He concludes, "The literal approach to the Bible claims not to interpret the Bible but merely to take it for what it obviously says. The words of the Bible in modern translation are taken to mean what they mean to the reader today. On this basis the Bible is said to condemn homosexuality in a number of places. But a historical-critical approach reads the Bible in its original historical and cultural context. This approach takes the Bible to mean, as best as can be determined, what its human authors intended to say in their own time and in their own way. Understood on its own terms, the Bible was not addressing our current questions about sexual ethics. The Bible does not condemn gay sex as we understand it today." Not some moral and social libertarian, however, he also has some words for all people, gay and straight, when it comes to issues of sexuality and morality:

"While the Bible makes no blanket condemnation of homogenital acts and even less of homosexuality, this does not mean that for lesbians and gay men anything goes. If they rely on the Bible for guidance and inspiration, lesbians and gay men will certainly feel bound by the core moral teachings of the Judeo-Christian tradition: be prayerful, reverence God, respect others, be loving and kind, be forgiving and merciful, be honest and be just. Work for harmony and peace. Stand up for the truth. Give of yourself for all that is good, and avoid all that you know to be evil. To do that is to follow God's way. To do that is to love God with your whole heart and soul. To do that is to be a true disciple of Jesus. . . . Living by the Bible, gay and lesbian people will submit to those severe moral requirements – and those requirements apply also to sex and to intimate relationships. That is all that can honestly be said about biblical teaching on homosexuality. If people would still seek to know outright if gay or lesbian sex in itself is good or evil, if homogenital acts per se are right or wrong, they will have to look somewhere else for an answer. For the fact of the matter is simple enough. The Bible never addresses that question. More than that, the Bible seems deliberately unconcerned about it."[17]

Oh and one more thing, Professor Helminiak is also an ordained Roman Catholic priest.

So things are not always what they seem. If we manage to claw our way through our prejudices, fears, preconceptions, and long-heard assumptions, the truth we often find shines like the stars above and navigates us to a far better, more loving, and far more Christ-like place. As I say, things are not always what they seem.

# ON THE FRONT LINE

I HAVE WRITTEN OF MY personal experience as a straight, Christian man who publicly changed his mind about gay issues, and I have written a long chapter presenting the Biblical arguments on the subject. But what of the millions of men and women who are gay and Christian? In much of the Western world, young people in particular have for the most part an easier time of being gay and of coming out than used to be the case. But that is in general society rather than within churches. This is not, of course, the truth in many other parts of the world, and we shall see in this section of the book how what we take for granted in North America or Western Europe is not universally true. But even where gay people are protected and even accepted, peer bullying can still be a major problem; social rejection and parental confusion or even hostility are all still sad realities. However, progress and positive change have been extraordinarily deep and rapid in recent years. The sombre irony of the situation is that in Christian homes – where compassion, acceptance, love, and understanding should be the norm – gay people tend to find the greatest opposition. We should never accept caricatures, and some of the reactions of Christian parents, siblings, and churches are kind and sensitive but, tragically, that is far from standard. A great deal depends on the location, the culture, and the church denomination involved and also on the age of the individuals who are gay, but the stories here represent a pretty fair cross-section of gay

Christian experiences. Some of the people I interviewed were happy and even eager to be named and gave me complete freedom to quote and identify them in this book, but others would speak to me only with a guarantee of anonymity. They come from the United States, Canada, Britain, Ireland, Lebanon, the Caribbean, and Australia and from most different brands of church. The only uniting factor is that they all come from Christian homes. Some have remained Christians, some became priests, some still have relationships with their families, some haven't spoken to their parents in many years, some left the Christian church long ago and are still angry and understandably hurt.[1] Although these stories do not directly address the theme of equal marriage, they deal specifically with the Christian response to homosexuality and gay people, which is largely the underpinning of the entire subject. Some of those interviewed here are now married to their same-sex partners but others are not. The issue is not whether they choose to wed but that they have the right to do so. I do not mind admitting that I often felt somewhat ashamed by what I heard.

This is also a chapter I need to put in context. Rather than comment on every story, I have generally allowed the subjects to speak for themselves. Most of this book consists of me, a straight man, speaking about gay issues, and I am convinced that at this point, around halfway through the book, we need to hear from those who are, as the chapter title suggests, on the front line. They have lived all this whereas I have merely written of it.

Aston was one of the first people to grant me an interview and also the first to insist that he not be named in full. He grew up just outside London, England, in a working-class suburb. He was born in 1964, had a brother who was two years older than him and a sister who was three years younger. His father was a police officer and his mother a nurse who worked part-time. They lived in a small but modern house, were comfortably off if not wealthy, and had what Aston calls "a loving, happy if not especially warm family set-up." Aston's parents were committed members of the Church of England and strongly identified with its evangelical and conservative wing. "On some issues they were surprisingly progressive," he says. "Both of them supported the ordination of women, and dad in particular was strongly opposed to the apartheid regime in South Africa. He'd been there on some sort of police trip a few years earlier and was absolutely appalled at what he saw. There was a fairly large Jewish community in the area where we lived and my parents were very pro-Jewish, very moved by what had happened in the Second World War. They voted Conservative but I think they always felt a little guilty about it. They hardly ever lost their temper, and I think my dad hit me maybe twice in my entire life, both times with an open hand on my leg and, to be honest, both times pretty well deserved. He was a good father for the most part, an honest cop who cared about people, a man who tried to live out his Christianity every day. My mum was softer, more emotional and gentle than my dad and spent more time with us. Understandable I suppose in that she was at home more than he was. No complaints though. They loved me and showed me their love."

Aston says he can't say when he first knew he was gay because he never felt anything else. "It wasn't that I suddenly realized that I was gay, more that I never felt non-gay, if that makes any sense. And it wasn't about sex, really – to be honest I've never been a very sexual person. I just found that I was emotionally attracted to certain boys at school, and I soon realized that it was not only emotional but romantic too. That can be disguised when you're a kid because everybody has best friends and guys who they spend a lot of time with. I would never have been physically intimate with a boy, I would have been terrified and wouldn't even have known what to do! All I knew was that when I was with certain boys – and one boy in particular – I felt complete, secure, and happy. In love. Yeah, in love. I can say it now, couldn't then. All through my teenage years I told nobody and I don't think anybody knew. Hold on, that might not be true. My sister might have had an idea. The church we attended wasn't some fire and brimstone place, and I don't remember homosexuality ever being mentioned except maybe in passing until the week I was about to go to university. There was something in the news about a gay issue in the church – I can't for the life of me remember exactly what it was – and the priest, the minister, at our church gave a full sermon about it. He wasn't cruel or nasty, and he spoke about love and understanding but he also made it clear that gay love and gay sex were terrible sins and that the Bible and the history of the church left no room for doubt. I felt that everybody was looking at me. They weren't, of course, but it felt that way. Awful.

"In the car home, it was my brother who brought up the sermon and made some stupid and insulting joke about being gay. My mother criticized him and said it was wrong to make fun of gay people and that as Christians we had to pray for them and do all we could to change them and help them be celibate and happy."

He pauses and looks at the ground, and I think to myself that he is going to ask me to stop the interview. He doesn't. "I think it was because I knew I was about to leave home for university and felt like an adult, felt more courage than before, I don't know. But I blurted out, louder and more angrily than I'd intended, that I was gay. My brother laughed. Nobody else did. Total silence all the way home and we were still a fifteen-minute drive away. It was like pins and needles were poking me, like one of those film shots when the camera suddenly focuses in on one person and everything else is blurred. We got home, silence. We all went in, more silence. Everybody went to various parts of the house, silence. I had my own room and sat in it and looked at my bag that was packed for the trip to university and began to cry." He cries now, and buries his face in his hands, sucking in air and weeping almost hysterically. I hold out my hand to him but he says it's okay and that it's just that he hasn't spoken about this in so long.

"Nothing happened for hours. I remember looking at my watch, it was a new one given to me by my parents as a present for getting into university. It was 5 p.m. The first person to speak to me was my mum a few hours later. She knocked on my door, told me dinner was ready. I sat in my room and didn't move. Then after 9 p.m. she came back and asked to speak to me. She sat on the bed but said nothing. Then she started to cry. I hugged her, she hugged me. She was shaking, physically shaking. She asked me if it was all true, was I sure, was there someone I was involved with, what was going on. She threw questions at me, fired them like a machine gun. I told her I was sure I was gay, always had been, that there was nobody I was seeing but that I intended to find someone if I could at university. Would I, she asked, come to meet with the minister – apparently they had already telephoned him. I knew they were going to ask that, I suppose, and I knew I had to agree. We went to his home that night and again drove in silence – my dad had not said a word to me since I had told them I was gay that morning. It was like someone had died or was dying.

"As I said, we didn't go to the church but the minister's home. He offered us tea. I remember joking and asking if it was gay tea – just a mixture of English humour and trying to diffuse the tension, I suppose. Nobody laughed, of course, but then it wasn't funny. He said we should start by praying and we did. I prayed every day so why not now? But it wasn't the usual type of prayers but a prayer to remove sexual darkness, to open our hearts to the truth of scripture, for me to know God's will. I can still hear those words as if it was yesterday and not more than thirty years ago. I wasn't angry, just resigned to it all. The minister then addressed me directly and told me I was loved by everybody there and loved by God and that God had made me perfect and in His image and that what is natural is of God, and sex between people of the same gender cannot be natural. He told me I was hurting my parents and family but most of all I was hurting God. I had no reply, no answers, no defence. Today I would have argued but not then, not when I was so young and had just told my family I was gay.

"I went off to university and my parents wrote letters to me every couple of days. They never came to visit me but on holidays I would go home. I know it sounds strange but we never spoke about it. It all became very cold at home, the love seemed to have disappeared. Nobody was ever unkind as such but every conversation, every interaction seemed to be taking place as if under water or in slow motion. I met my partner, Steve, at university in the second year and told my mum and dad. I would never have asked to have him stay with me at home but I did ask if he could visit. They said no. I am still with him all these years later but my dad never met him – Dad died in 2000 of a heart attack. Mum met Steve once but was not friendly; my brother and sister blame me for my dad's premature death and say that my mum also holds me responsible. I see my brother and sister every now and again and call my mum on her birthday but that's about it. I've tried to rebuild the relationship but she has become very closed and extremely religious. She's joined some sort of evangelical church now apparently. I left the Church long ago. I believe in God, I love the teachings of Jesus, but too many of His followers believe my union with the man I love is immoral and wrong and I just haven't got the strength left to deal with all that.

"The crazy thing is that Steve, my partner, became a cop after university and served in the same police station as my dad had served years earlier. I wish they could have met. It might have changed so many things. I wish they could have met."

I heard many stories similar to this in researching this book. The key emotion is often regret and frustration rather than anger. Regret because the people I spoke to knew that it could all so easily have been different, and frustration because they were generally convinced that it could so easily have been different and happier.

Pearce J. Carefoote was more than willing to be completely open about who he is and to be specific in his experience. He is fifty-four years old, an ordained Anglican priest in Canada, and a senior librarian at the world-renowned Thomas Fisher Rare Book Library at the University of Toronto. Before that, he was a Roman Catholic priest. He studied at the Catholic University of Louvain in Belgium, where was awarded a Doctorate of Sacred Theology in Church History and successfully defended (*summa cum laude*) his dissertation: "Augustine, the Pelagians and the Papacy: An Examination of the Political and Theological Implications of Papal Involvement in the Pelagian Controversy" and also gained a licentiate in Sacred Theology. He also has a master's in Divinity. He taught religious studies at McMaster University in Canada and in the Roman Catholic high school system and is a frequently published academic. Between 1988 and 1990, he was associate pastor at St. Mary's Roman Catholic Church in Brampton, Ontario.

"There wasn't a moment when I absolutely knew I was gay but in another way I always knew and tried to pretend otherwise, tried to squish it down. I was raised Catholic, always believed in God, felt I had a vocation, and decided to enter the seminary. I was twenty-one, just about to enter, and I was in New York with a friend. I knew I felt things for him, felt a certain way about him. I went to St. Patrick's Cathedral and went to confession to tell the priest what I was feeling. He was very kind and very understanding and said that as long as I didn't act on my feelings, I had nothing to worry about. So that's what I did. But of course it's not that easy. I prayed and I struggled and I did all I could to do the right thing. Thing is, I knew for a fact that maybe half of the men around me in the seminary were gay – I've no idea how many were celibate but I know that not all of them were. In 1983, just before the Pope visited Canada, the rector of the seminary thought he should address the issue because he was aware of how many of his students were gay and that there were of course gay people in the congregation too. He did it well and with great sensitivity, but some of the more conservative students there became upset and made sure it all became very public. There was an apostolic visitation, an investigation, lots of media, and a number of seminarians were removed and the rector was dismissed. So here we had a genuine, serious attempt to deal with the issue honestly but the backlash was just too strong. As a result of that, everything was hidden again.

"My being gay was part of a process really. Bit by bit I came to accept it more. I would go to confession, pray for forgiveness but the process continued. I went to study in Belgium and told one of my teachers about my sexuality and he sent me to see a Catholic psychologist. Then I came back to Canada for the ordination in New Brunswick of an old friend from a large Catholic family and I noticed that during the Mass his brother didn't go up to receive communion. I asked why and was told he was gay. So I spoke to the brother and he told me, 'I don't go where I'm not welcome.' Then I looked around at the number of us in the sanctuary who were ordained and I knew who were gay and I also knew some of them certainly weren't celibate – to be honest, at this point I hadn't been completely celibate – and realized that this just wasn't right.

"In the summer of 1994, I came back to Toronto and went to see the then Archbishop of Toronto, Aloysius Ambrozic, and told him about my feelings and asked if I could take some time away to think and reflect. He was not at all sympathetic or understanding and gave me very little time. It wasn't a friendly or pleasant experience. He did say that I was the first gay priest he'd ever met, which is incredible really. I may have been the only priest he'd ever met who admitted to be being gay but I can assure you he knew and worked with many, many gay priests. He then said that if he'd known 'what' I was – 'what' I was, not 'who' I was – he'd never have educated me in the first place. He asked if my superiors had known, and I told him that they had. He said that they should never have ordained me even though I was then totally celibate. So he was telling me that celibacy wasn't the issue, the only thing that matters was that I was gay. I left the office, and a week later I received a letter from the chancellor suspending me from my orders and from my office and that was it. That was an incredibly quick process and they obviously wanted me gone.

"I continued to go to Mass though because I was still a Catholic, but now I would have panic attacks because I was so worried at how people would treat me if they knew, and I was also worried that I would be recognized. I hadn't outed myself to any members of my family at this point so they didn't know why I had left and I was concerned people might realize what was going on. When I did tell my family, they were wonderful and very accepting. I told my elderly, very Irish and very Catholic aunt. She asked me if I was happy. I said I was. Then she said it was fine. I told her I met someone, a man I would eventually marry. She asked me if he was Catholic. I said he was. She then asked if he was Irish. I said he was. Good then, she said, you'll be fine. I learned very soon that what mattered was my faith in God and in Jesus and in the mercy of Christ, not in the Church. I have to admit that I had been a pretty judgemental person before all that but not now. I've even managed to forgive the archbishop and to forgive the Roman Catholic Church.

"I sincerely want to believe that there can be change in the Catholic Church and the priests who I still know are men who would change the teaching on same-sex relationships immediately if they had that power. But, sadly, they don't. I thought when Pope Francis first arrived and spoke out about kindness and tolerance that change might be possible but the realities of the job have made him more circumspect and even hostile at times. Look, let's be honest about this: there are lots of gay priests out there and some of them live in agony because they don't want to be celibate. Because of this they sometimes turn to abuse – abuse of drugs, abuse of alcohol, abuse of power and, tragically, abuse of young boys too. The Church can't have it both ways. If celibacy is a gift, and I believe it is whatever one's sexuality, it can't then be imposed on people and certainly can't be forced on every person who is gay."

What Pearce doesn't say because he is too modest is that he was considered one of the most gifted young priests of his generation and great things were expected of him. It's the tragedy of the Roman Catholic Church on this issue that he has indeed fulfilled that greatness, but not as a Roman Catholic.


Damian is from Sligo in Ireland and is a young and dynamic-looking eighty years old. He grew up in a large family where some of his siblings were taken in by what he was always told were aunts and uncles but he was never entirely sure. His father drove trucks around the country and his mother was at home. "To be honest," he says, "she was more accurately in bed rather than at home. Fourteen kids in the small house and at least three others sent away. But the idea that there was no love and that Dad would drink and beat up Mum – well, that was nothing like my upbringing. They loved each other very much, and Dad never even looked at another woman. Problem was he looked at Mum too much, and I think they sincerely desired each other. With Catholic teaching on birth control and abortion and the culture of the time, combined with their fertility, she was always bloody pregnant. No money, no room, no new clothes, no clean running water some of the time but no violence and no arguing really. We were happy, didn't know any other way." He throws back his head and laughs out loud. "Did I know I was gay? No way. I didn't even know what gay was, what homosexual was, even what sex was. It sounds mad, doesn't it, that in a house where there was a lot of sex going on and a lot of its consequences were so obvious – but I tell you that sex was a blur to us and nobody had ever met a gay person. When I look back now, I suppose some of the priests – there were a lot of them, I can tell you – were gay and I am pretty certain some of the nuns too but we never thought about it much. I was never sexually abused by a priest but I was hit by them a lot and I've a feeling some of them got off on it. In fact, the only violence I ever saw from an adult was not from Dad or Mum but from a father or a sister.

"I joined the army, the British Army, for a job. I wasn't political and couldn't care less about Ireland or Britain but there was a job in the British Army and for an Irishman it didn't pay badly. I learned a lot in the army. I learned how to fire a gun, how to polish my boots properly, how to sleep for five hours a night." He laughs again, always more self-mocking than at others. "I also learned how to love God and how to love other men. No, I don't mean everybody was gay but some were and I realized that I was too. You had to be extremely discreet and careful in those days, not so much because of the fear of being beaten up by other soldiers but because you'd have been thrown out without any money or references. The man I got to know well, who I grew to love, was the son of European Jews who had come to London before the Second World War. Not many Jews in the army but lots of bloody Irishmen." He laughs again. "I never found out why he joined but I'd never met anyone like him. Our relationship wasn't very physical, more loving and close. Then his parents died very quickly, in the space of a month or two from one another, and he was given a compassionate discharge. I tried to keep in contact but he seemed to have changed, didn't want to know me any more, and back then there were no cellphones or e-mail. The strange thing is that it was the unit padre, the Church of England minister, who came to my rescue. There may have been a Catholic priest around but I'd had enough of the Catholic Church years earlier. This guy though, he must have known what was going on and he was so kind and gentlemanly with me. Without ever mentioning sex or gays, he told me he was there if ever I needed him. We did chat. It helped me. That was nice.

"I left the army eventually but that chaplain had left a mark. I got a job, found a place to live, started attending church actually. I was happy. I had relationships with men but wasn't interested in anything long-term, and back then you could be in real trouble if you were caught. Assaults, prison, blackmail. By God, I knew men who were arrested and sent to prison for 'indecency.' Good men some of them, men who had sacrificed a lot for their country. I then met Nick at my church, we became an item, we fell in love, and we lived together. There is no way that other people at the church didn't know about us because we spent years there and were involved in services, parties, fundraising, helping out, prayer circles, and all that. We weren't flamboyant or ostentatious but of course they knew. Then Nick was diagnosed with cancer and he declined so quickly, so horribly, in front of my eyes and in front of the congregation's eyes. I sometimes had trouble visiting him in hospital and was often asked if I were a relative or not, you know the sort of thing. Then he died."

There is no laughter this time but only tears. His cheeks become swamped with crying, bisected with a sorrow that looks like it was disguised and held back for so long. When he speaks again, his Irish accent is thicker and stronger. He suddenly looks his age, and it's as though he speaks for that entire older generation of gay men who suffered so deeply at the hands of the Christian church.

"I went to the church, to the deacons, to the minister and asked them for help with the funeral and all that went with it. All they wanted to know was whether he had died of AIDS. I told them we had been faithful partners for years and no, of course it wasn't AIDS. I knew they didn't believe me. They were obviously unwilling to arrange the funeral, and suddenly my supposed friends were not around for me any more and I was alone. One of the deacons gave me two pamphlets. One was about grieving and the other was about the sin of homosexuality. It was like a second loss, a slap around the face after being smashed in the stomach.

"I never set foot in the place again or in any other church. I'm told that things have changed in some churches today, I know there are gay churches, I know some progressive churches are very welcoming to gay people but I can't forgive the bastards. I still believe in God but I suppose I don't love Him any longer. If He is all-powerful, why does He allow His churches to be the way they are? I'm sorry, I don't mean to be nasty and I know many Christians are not like that but my lover, my partner, my Nick was tossed away like garbage by the people he had worshipped with for years. Community? Community, my arse!"

Most of the gay people I spoke to for this chapter and indeed for the entire book were men. I struggled to convince gay women to allow me to interview them. There are numerous reasons for their reluctance but it's partly because – in my experience at least – they often felt more betrayed by organized Christianity than did gay men. That is certainly what Cindy told me. She is thirty-five years old and grew up in Fort Worth, Texas, in a Southern Baptist family. She is an only child and was raised by her mother after her father died from lung cancer when Cindy was still a teenager. She and her mother were extremely close and loving and she describes her childhood as intensely happy, the only blemish being the tragic death of her father – a senior manager at a department store. "I didn't want to be gay. I hated the feelings I had and completely accepted that the Bible condemned homosexual behaviour and that even same-sex attraction was a sign of my broken nature and my sin. I'd dated boys but it never came to anything, and when I was seventeen I met a girl from Ohio who was working at our church. I'd never met anybody like her and I fell in love. She was training to be a missionary, and while I am pretty sure she felt the same way about me as I did about her, she told me when I mentioned it that I had to resist everything I was feeling and find a boy to love and marry. I've never seen her again and have no idea if she came out. I hope she's happy whatever her decision. After that it was like a door had been opened and I pretty much knew I was gay. But gay in Texas, in a Southern Baptist church, almost twenty years ago, was not easy. But if I'm honest about it all, it wasn't so much other people, it was me. The church was the centre of my existence, and I had been told all of my life not only that homosexuality was sinful but that gay people were trying to change our lives and our country and that we had to be on alert. I know, crazy! It was less we didn't like gays than we didn't know any. No, let me try that again. Not hate perhaps but incredible dislike and suspicion. And in spite of that, here I was feeling attracted to other women. I thought it must be a dent, something wrong, maybe something I'd grow out of eventually. I told my mum – we were close – and she cried with me. She told me not to worry and that we would sort it all out. We went to see our minister, and he said it was beyond his field and his expertise. He referred us to a specialist in Dallas, and we went to see him. He told us about conversion or reparative therapy, and I began to see him every week. Nice guy, really, and while he was a Christian, he spoke a lot in secular terms about parental imbalance and trauma and how it wasn't really my fault at all. He spoke a lot about sex too but I told him it was less the sex than the companionship. He had me do mental and spiritual exercises, imagine being with a boy on a perfect date, asked me to look ahead and ask myself what I wanted and what was real and what was imagined. This went on for more than a year and my poor mother was paying for all this. All it did was make me angry and scared.

"The first time I tried to kill myself was with pills. I can't honestly tell if you if I was serious or not. I think I was – I took enough to do the job but then I also knew my mum was always home at a certain time in the day and that she would probably find me. They got me to the hospital and pumped my stomach. Here's a weird thing – I felt safer and more relaxed in that hospital than I had been in two years at home. I got out, went to another, different Christian therapist and he was more aggressive than the first one. He told me how much pain I was causing and how I had disappointed my family and God. I tried to kill myself again, and when that failed and I recovered, I left home and went to Atlanta and then to New York. The reason I left, the reason I never tried to harm myself ever again, was that the second time I was in hospital, the nurse looking after me was a Christian, a Quaker, and she told me I was loved by God and that I was meant to be gay. She said I was perfect as a gay woman and that it was other Christians and other people who had to change to accept me and not me who had to change to please them. I had never in my life been told that before. Never. I went to church in Atlanta where the congregation was mostly gay, and now in New York I go to an Episcopalian church where nobody cares if I am gay or not. I go with my wife – she's another Texan girl but her family and community was more understanding than mine – and we're very happy and very Christian. My mum comes to see us sometimes and is very fond of my wife but she doesn't want us to visit her in Fort Worth – hey, I understand why and I know it's not easy. Little steps. Little Christian steps."


Tom Decker is forty-seven years old, was born in Austria but grew up in Brisbane, Australia, and is one of three former Roman Catholic priests included in this chapter. His family was Roman Catholic but they attended Mass only five or six times a year. Tom became a Roman Catholic priest but left the priesthood and the Catholic Church. He is now an ordained priest in the Anglican Church. "I noticed when I was about ten years old that I was somehow different from the other boys but I didn't know what that difference was. I knew absolutely nothing about homosexuality or what this was all about and what I felt. I did know that I was far more interested in close friendships with my schoolmates than in meeting girls but I didn't know what this meant at the time. There was nothing sexual about it at all, and initially it didn't worry me in any way whatsoever. After about three years, my mates didn't seem so interested in doing things together because they wanted to chase girls and to find girlfriends. It was then that I realized that there was something genuinely different about me and that something was going on. I suppose I became a little annoyed at my schoolmates and angry that anything had to change because I had been so happy but still I didn't have any idea about what being gay was and who I was. Remember, I grew up in the reign of Sir Joh Bjelke-Petersen, who was premier of Queensland and a strong evangelical and a staunch homophobe who back then spoke of 'homosexual conspiracies.' But this was also the time of the onslaught of the AIDS epidemic.

"It was about that time that I realized for certain that I was not attracted to girls but I couldn't bring my brain round to the fact that I was attracted to boys. It was just something I didn't want to consider. By the time I was sixteen I did know some friends who were gay, even though I didn't regard myself as being gay, and on one weekend spring evening they invited me to go with them to Fortitude Valley, the very small area in the city that was something resembling a gay village. There was a gay bar there, and they wanted to have a few drinks and to dance, nothing sexual really. I wasn't yet seventeen and wasn't of drinking age so at around 9:30 or 10 p.m. I decided to go home on my own. I was walking towards the bus when I heard someone or maybe a group of people say something like 'There's another of those fags!' The next thing I knew I woke up in hospital with thirty-eight stitches in my head after someone had taken a shovel to me. I couldn't tell my parents what had happened so I told them I had been robbed. The police came to see me and asked me if I might have any idea why this had happened to me, and I think they were asking if I was gay and it had been a homophobic attack. I said I had no idea. They found the shovel but it had been wiped clean so the person or persons who did it were never found. But it convinced me that I couldn't tell anyone the way I felt and who I was. There I was lying in a hospital and suddenly certain that I could never be allowed to be gay.

"I think the whole idea of joining the Roman Catholic priesthood was born out of that assault. I knew I had been targeted for who and what I was and never wanted to be in that situation ever again. So I pushed everything to do with sexuality away from me, and as a defence mechanism I completely suppressed my entire sexuality. I'd also known Catholic priests in the parish and they were good men. I suppose that within a year of all that happening, I realized that the easiest way out for me and the way to avoid telling my parents that I wasn't going to get married and to have to explain why was to become a celibate priest, so I studied hard, I worked hard, and I was ordained.

"My religious order were starting a university in India, and they wanted me to be professor of the Old Testament at that university. In order to be fully qualified, I had to get my Ph.D. in Old Testament studies and so they sent me to the University of Toronto. But coming from a very sheltered environment in Australia to a big city like Toronto, I became extremely curious about what was going on. Suddenly things weren't hidden or denied and so much was open. I remember attending my first Pride parade but I was so terrified of being recognized that I walked a few blocks away from it, sort of parallel but not too close. Funny, really, but also rather sad. Then I got more and more curious and eventually met someone, and it was then that I knew I had to come out and had to stop living such a lie. It just seemed wrong to not tell the truth, and I thought that my superiors would appreciate and understand that. That's not what happened though. I told them I had to leave the priesthood, and that didn't go over too well at all, let me tell you. First they tried to convince me to stay and were quite nice about it all but once they knew my mind was made up, they started with threats and abuse. That didn't work either so at that point they offered me a double life: if I remained a priest, they said, I could live this double life. I could have a small parish, not one in the big city, and live with my partner but had to be very quiet about it all and never tell anyone. I was shocked at what they were suggesting and realized that this wasn't about me but about filling a vacancy and keeping up the numbers. I knew then I had to live my life authentically and with integrity. I had to leave. Look, I know other men have gone along with such offers and still do so and I am not sitting in judgement over those priests who have said yes but I simply could not reconcile it all. It just wasn't for me.

"When I came out, I felt it as a huge relief. There was nothing more to hide and I could be me. Don't get me wrong, though – those first few weeks were gruesome and horrific. I had nightmares, I didn't know if I would ever find a job or if anybody would ever talk to me again. As a Catholic priest, you are put on a pedestal and looked up to and I suppose people thought I had let them down. Though at the same time I also had friends who were very kind and who said they respected me for being truthful. I felt I couldn't just walk away from the priesthood; I wanted to do the whole thing properly so I commissioned Rome for a laicization. Under Pope John Paul II that was almost unheard of and could take an enormous amount of time but I got mine in six months, which was unprecedented. I think Rome must have thought that they should get rid of a gay priest because this was the height of revelations about the abuse scandal in the Church, and for many Catholics being gay means being a pedophile and they thought there might be a scandal in the making so wanted me out as quickly as possible. Ridiculous but that's how it was.

"Finding a job wasn't easy – a former priest, recently out as a gay man – and in the end I became a gun-carrying cop in Toronto. Funny, really, but they didn't care about what I had been. It worked out well, and eventually I became police liaison officer for the LGBT community. But I missed my vocation and my call to ministry and there was this need in me to return to organized religion. I felt incomplete and as though there was something drastically missing or empty. I had been attending the Metropolitan Community Church which is gay-centred and so accepting and welcoming and eventually I asked to be ordained there, so in 2010 they recognized my former Roman Catholic orders and I worked as a minister in Toronto and then in Rochester, New York. It had been so painful being denied the right to celebrate the Eucharist and being told that I was, in effect, not welcome at the table. Now I was welcome, now I was welcome. Look, a lot of Catholic priests are gay, maybe a third or whatever I don't know, and there are some priests who are very well-known in the gay scene but, again, I am not going to sit in judgement and not going to name names.

"As for those people who say that you cannot be a Christian and be an active gay person, I am afraid that the scriptures and especially the Old Testament, my field of expertise, just don't bear that out at all. If you cherry-pick the Bible and take verses out of context, you get into very serious trouble. We see this in the story of Sodom and in Leviticus – people just don't understand what is going on in these stories and place them outside of the understanding and meaning of the author and what was really being said. I mean, have they actually read the list of 'abominations'? If so, I am pretty sure that I will receive the death penalty for wearing what I am right now, probably a mixture of cloths! But it's very hard for evangelicals and fundamentalists to accept that the Bible was written over a space of a thousand years. I mean, look at the case of slavery – the Bible doesn't condemn it but we most certainly do today. Or take the relationship between David and Jonathan, which if you read it in the Hebrew is clearly a homoerotic relationship. There is a two-word combination that occurs in the poem where David laments the death of Jonathan that only occurs elsewhere in scripture in The Song of Songs, which is so clearly about sex that rabbis as late as the first century debated removing it from the canon because it was considered pornographic. The entire homophobic approach simply doesn't fit with accepted Biblical scholarship. Can we be Christian and gay? Oh please! I married my husband in 2011 and faith is at the centre of our lives. We pray together, we couldn't do otherwise."


Bobby is from Kampala, Uganda, and is twenty-seven years old. She comes from a middle-class Anglican Christian family though her mother converted from Islam when she married her father. She has two brothers and one sister and gained a degree in economics from a university in the British Midlands – she insisted that I not provide precise details because she is frightened of the possible consequences for her family and because she promised her father that she would not, to use his words, "embarrass and disgrace" the family. She returned to Uganda after university but left again in 2014 and has no plans to return unless the politics of the country and the Ugandan church's attitudes toward homosexuality change radically and gay people are given acceptance and protection.

"I grew up with a certain privilege, and compared to most people in Uganda we were wealthy and secure. It was rather idyllic, really, in that we had a nanny and a gardener, the climate was gorgeous, my parents were loving and considerate, and I went to a private school that was very English. I always thought of myself as a bit of a tomboy – do people still use that term? – and I suppose people around me thought the same thing. It was all a bit of a cliché really. I played sport with the boys, climbed trees, didn't like wearing dresses, and so on. There was never anything sexual or romantic in my life, and I don't remember even really knowing what lesbianism was. I'd heard about homosexuality from one of the ministers in church and from an American who came to our particular church to speak about it and what a threat it was and how much damage it had done in the United States but I thought for some reason that only men could be gay; it wasn't until university that I found out that homosexual didn't mean love between men but love for someone like yourself. We never discussed these things at home but when we went to church, and we were a very Anglican family, the subject seemed to come up again and again. On the one hand we were told that it was a foreign problem and that Ugandans weren't really gay, and on the other hand we were warned that gays were everywhere and a threat to everything we cared about. I always remember my little brother saying to my father, 'Daddy, monsters aren't real, are they? But homosexuals are real, aren't they?' It was like that: monsters, gays, terrorists, all the same I suppose.

"It was only when my friends began to date that I thought something might be different about me. I just didn't want to go out with boys. Not with girls either, though – I just wasn't interested in dating. I was about fifteen then and this went on for about two years. Then one night at a party, we all got a bit drunk and that was easy for me because my family were pretty strict and I'd hardly any experience of alcohol at all. I was waiting to go to the bathroom and started talking to another girl who was in the line and then we were the only two there and suddenly she kissed me. Nothing aggressive or even passionate. Just a little kiss. She apologized quickly, said she had got the wrong idea, and pleaded with me not to say anything. She must have thought I was offended or frightened and that I would tell someone. I can't quite remember what I said but I know I walked away, went home, and felt so good about it, so good about myself, so calm, so complete really. It felt as though this was what life and happiness were supposed to feel like and that what was supposed to have happened had happened.

"I asked around my friends about this girl and found out who she was. Weeks later – because I was naïve and a bit scared and totally inexperienced – I waited by her home and then spoke to her. From then on we were, well, best friends, I suppose. I don't think we ever did anything more than hugged and held hands. The occasional kiss, maybe, but it was so innocent. That was all. So without guilt, so lovely, so charming. I didn't think of myself as gay or a lesbian or homosexual or anything. All I knew was that I was happy and that was all. Then I wasn't. She was hit by a car and killed and the driver didn't even stop. Now, it could have been an accident and I know I might sound paranoid but I am convinced that she was killed because of who and what she was. She came from a poorer background than mine was, and a few girls, and more boys, who were gay from her sort of background had been beaten, raped, or murdered at around that time. I was sure then and I am sure now that my first love, this good and sweet and entirely blameless young woman, was killed like an animal because she was gay. You might think it's the grief speaking but you don't know Africa and you don't know Uganda.

"I went to see the priest at our church because he had known our family for a long time and I trusted him. What a fool I was. He blamed her for what had happened and said I had been led astray and even though he had promised not to do so he went to tell my parents. They were angry but not violent. They said I was imagining she was murdered in just the same way that I was imagining that I was a lesbian. It sounds ridiculous as I retell all this but my punishment was to be sent away to a university in Britain so I could be free of what was influencing me in Uganda. Most Ugandan gays can't even afford to leave the town, and I was being paid to leave the country and have a great time at a university! In Britain, of course, I came out as gay completely and almost immediately and have had various relationships. I went back home afterwards and told my family about who I was and they said I was no longer welcome at home but that they would continue to support me financially. They were heartbroken. I know I should be angry with them but I can't be and I still love them. It's so hard for them because they have been told for so many years by priests and ministers and missionaries that homosexuality is evil and wrong. I blame the Church and I blame American Christians a great deal too. I saw the influence and the money that came from the United States around all of this. I'm not saying that native Ugandan Christians aren't guilty, because they are and homophobia is part of our country's religious history, but the Church in the West should be trying to help us and not making things worse. Do I still miss her? Every single day."


Maurice Tomlinson was born in Jamaica in 1971 and is one of the West Indies' leading gay activists. He has two brothers and was educated in Jamaica as well as Italy and North America. He is a highly respected attorney, academic, and speaker. At one point earlier in his life, he was a successful and popular flight attendant with Air Jamaica but left after one of his bosses told him that some passengers had complained that he might be gay and then recommended that to counter this perception he "stand in front of a mirror and try to be more macho and deepen his voice." When he explains all this to me, Tomlinson laughs: "I mean, 75 per cent of all male flight attendants are gay, and this woman who was telling me to appear more straight had flown all over the world but didn't seem to realize that straight men were the exceptions in her profession." In 2012, he received the David Kato award for human rights activism for his work in the Caribbean on behalf of gay rights. The award is named after a Ugandan gay activist who was murdered. In 2013, Tomlinson became a founding member of Dwayne's House, named after Jamaican Dwayne Jones, a transgendered sixteen-year-old who was beaten, stabbed, shot, and then run over after attending a party in female clothes. The eponymous house was established to help feed, protect, and help homeless gay teenagers who have been thrown out of their homes and often live in the Kingston sewers and have to prostitute themselves to raise money for food. Tomlinson has worked extensively to challenge the anti-homosexual laws in

Jamaica and still visits regularly to speak and advise. In 2012, he married his partner and as a consequence received numerous death threats.

"Look, there is a large Christian movement out there which claims that it can cure people of their homosexuality and their homosexual feelings. The whole thing involves meetings, lots of prayer, and a great deal of counselling. I should know because for quite a long time I was part of such a group and it even met at my home. None of it worked, of course, and in the end I had relationships with two of the men in the group. One of them went on to become clinically depressed and the other has left his family. These groups do enormous harm and in a way cause or did cause the greater spread of AIDS because they lead people to hide who they are, what they feel, and whom they love. In Jamaica, more than 80 per cent of people openly and proudly self-identify as homophobic, violence against gay people is common, and there have been cases of gay men murdered with machetes. Just awful, just awful.

"I was raised in Montego Bay by parents who were members of the Open Bible Church, a Pentecostal denomination based in Des Moines, Iowa. Of course homosexuality was condemned but generally it just wasn't discussed. We knew gay people and even had relatives who were gay but we didn't ask and they didn't tell. They had friends, close friends, of the same gender and we left it at that. Montego Bay is the centre of the Jamaican tourism industry so we saw many gay tourists and so on. It wasn't a good situation but it wasn't that bad, I suppose. More middle-class and educated people could rise quite high even though they were gay and in the rural and inner-city areas those who were gay were seen as products of the community, of being one of their own, and were not persecuted as such. Then in the 1970s, 80s, and into the 90s, the televangelists started to do their thing. Jamaica was just turning to full cable and these guys were everywhere. They were all American at first and then we had the local clones of them and they spewed the most incredible, violent, vile anti-gay stuff. It was the time of the AIDS paranoia, and these people not only condemned homosexuality but also said that AIDS was a gay disease and that it was God's punishment for being gay. Gays spread AIDS, they said, so the only way to eradicate AIDS was to eradicate gays. That was when the terrible violence and persecution really got going. My mum, for example, had been raised Anglican and tolerant but that was all gone now for most people. The televangelists were on the television all the time pumping this vitriol into the country and they in turn influenced entire generations. Everybody in Jamaica is raised in church, you see, so that even our musicians – who are incredibly popular – have injected this homophobia from the Christian televangelists into their music. We have the most anti-gay songs per capita in the entire world, and as there are no quiet zones in the country – music is everywhere – enormous numbers of people hear this stuff and embrace it. Society became marinated in homophobia, and when politicians saw how popular homophobia was, they adopted [the viewpoint] so as to be popular and get elected and it became the perfect storm.

"I knew I was different from the earliest stage. I was looking at a photo the other day and there were my two brothers standing ramrod straight, looking at the camera, and then there was me, standing like a doll or something" – he laughs out loud – "and I suppose it was obvious even back then. My mum said she knew when I was twelve that I was gay but she had hoped that I would change or be 'cured.' I tried, I honestly tried, to change and be like other people. I dated girls and then even married a lovely Catholic girl and we had a son together. My wife knew I was a gay, she had a gay brother, but thought she could change me and thought that our marriage would be some sort of panacea. It was all very sad. I was a good father but we had to separate in the end because I knew I could never be able to show my son his parents being intimate or romantic together and that this would damage him. My wife was willing for us to stay together and live in different rooms but that would have done so much harm to our boy. I was scared that I would grow up resenting my son because I had stayed in a marriage where I was unhappy and living something untrue. I've seen these unhealthy marriages way too many times, I'm afraid.

"I'm a Christian, and I have never left the faith in spite of all of the hatred, the abuse, the violence, and the venom. I may have left the church but not the faith. The message of Christ was inclusion and love for the marginalized, in particular, and I still believe that so strongly. I have experienced too many events in my life that cannot be explained, miracles I suppose, for me to leave the Christian faith. I attended a gay-centred church, a place of healing and acceptance, and I now worship as an Anglican. I feel loved and welcomed, but I do believe that there will be a schism between the African and the Western churches over the gay issue, and maybe that's a good thing in the end. As for forgiving those people on television who caused so much pain and harm and are still doing so, I know it's not very Christian of me but I can't do that. Not unless they acknowledge what they have done and see that their words have led to people being beaten and killed and to parents throwing out ten-year-old children to the streets because they think they are gay. They feel justified in these terrible actions by the televangelists and yet these people still call themselves followers of Jesus. Unless they admit to what they have done, I can't forgive them but up to now they not only won't admit it but they are incredibly proud of it. It breaks my heart."


Grant Jahnke is a gay man who has been in a committed relationship for more than twenty-seven years. He is sixty-six years old and comes originally from western Canada but now lives in Toronto. "I served for a mostly wonderful thirteen years as a priest in a Roman Catholic religious order. The church that inspired me and drew me to the priesthood was the church of Pope John XXIII. It presented a vision that was aligned with my understanding of – and my experience of – Jesus Christ. I see this kind of radiance shining once again in the humble, honest, and fearless presence of Pope Francis. Among the several reasons that led me to a painful departure from the vocation which I had firmly believed to be a lifetime commitment was the rampant duplicity I discovered among my brother priests in the area of fidelity to the vow of chastity. So often it was those who were the most dogmatic about 'upholding the Church's teaching' who were the most spectacularly sexually active. The brazen hypocrisy of these men and the complicity of all the gay clergy, celibate and otherwise, in the Church's persecution of other homosexuals is what led, indeed pushed, me to risk greater congruence in my own life.

"Growing up spiritually also means humble acknowledgement of the fact that the 'truth' is not black and white. I must therefore acknowledge with gratitude that despite my disaffection for so many of the men in the Catholic hierarchy, as I look back on my life the men who have been the greatest influence on me for the good, and who have been my most significant role models, have been Roman Catholic priests. And predictably, in these times when ideologies are gaining ascendance and polarization is a strategy of maintaining control, a firestorm has been unleashed, which is pretty much like what happened to Jesus. Thank God that the Church, for all its breathtaking collusion with the 'powers and principalities,' cannot separate us from the love of Christ.

"I knew from a pretty early age, seven or eight I suppose, that I was attracted to boys and in particular to a neighbouring kid who was four or five years older than me. But that was also when I started to know, or to think, that it wasn't acceptable to be that way so I buried it pretty substantially for decades. My career became being straight. Seriously, I had to stop doing the things that I loved to do and the things that made me happy. I stopped dancing, stopped going to theatre, stopped doing all the things that a boy in Alberta wasn't supposed to do and to like. My family was part Catholic, part Anglican, a bit Mennonite, and I was only attracted to the Catholic priesthood by a beautiful serendipity. I went to graduate school to work in the field of Canadian studies but there I met members of the Oblates of Mary Immaculate, a wonderful Catholic religious community and I was enormously impressed with them. Here were down-to-earth men with a real spirituality, great guys. Over several years, I was drawn to them, they influenced me a great deal, they were some of the best human beings I have ever met. Over a period of five years, I was drawn closer to them so I tried a year at their novitiate, I studied theology, and through a long process of discernment I opted for the priesthood. The Oblates of Mary Immaculate were a very progressive order and dealt with issues of sexuality and celibacy in a way that was very real.

We didn't discuss homosexuality a lot but it was discussed, it wasn't simply ignored. Frankly, I didn't know any other gay people, really, and I was so grateful to God for giving me this vocation and for finding me a place where I didn't have to be alone. You see, if I'd been straight I would love to have been married but as I couldn't be, this was another way to be part of something bigger than me. I remember telling this to my spiritual director and, yes, in some ways it was a choice between being gay and being celibate. I opted for the latter. I was ordained in 1981, and it was the most blessed day of my life.

"Why did I leave? There were several vectors that stacked up. I began to be increasingly uncomfortable after the Church retrenched with Pope John Paul II and I wasn't sure if this Pope spoke for me and represented my theology. Some of the things I was being asked to support and proclaim I simply couldn't say and do, I couldn't stand up and argue for them. It just seemed so clear that much of it was contrary to the teaching and the manner of Jesus. I began to feel personally uncomfortable having to do the bidding of Rome and there was never any opportunity for conversation or rebuttal. Everything seemed to be going backwards. Linked to this was, as I said earlier, the duplicity of my brother priests. I don't mean the Oblates of Mary Immaculate but elsewhere. I suppose I wasn't prepared for the reality of the Church as a whole, and when I worked in the diocese I was genuinely shocked by the opportunities that were there for gay sex and how the priests I met who were actually engaged in it were so reluctant to discuss it and justify it. I'd say that at least 50 per cent of Roman Catholic clergy are gay, and it could be higher. Thing is, I was still celibate at this time and I remained so until I left the priesthood. I took my vows seriously and tried to live up to them. Yet sex was offered to me quite frequently in the priesthood, and my experience was that the guys who have left the priesthood and came out as being gay and are now in long-term relationships were the ones who played by the rules and remained celibate. It was the ones who were sexual, sometimes promiscuous, who have tended to remain priests and still pretend and even defend Church teaching against homosexuality.

"I was happy as a priest, very happy indeed. But I'd read a book called *A Disturbed Peace* about being an Irish Catholic homosexual and I realized that I'd changed my world view. You see, the author's experience was so much like mine, and he sounded so normal and healthy. I wrote to him, and he responded with a long, lovely letter. I thought that if there was one other person like me there surely had to be others, there had to be more! What had changed was that I realized for the first time in my life that a happy, healthy committed relationship with another man was possible. This was a huge shift in my world view.

"Then one morning a couple of years later, I was driving in my car and I looked to the clouds and thought, I remembered I suppose, that I always wanted to be in a relationship and in a home and that was my primary desire and I can't just wait in the priesthood waiting for it to come to me. I knew I had to come clean, to make myself available, to be honest. That was the key moment. I loved my job, I knew I was respected, and I was liked as a priest, but within a year of that morning I went to see my superior and told him I had to leave. I know that some of my deepest friends in the order were deeply affected by what I did even though I wasn't as explicit as I could have been and I certainly never wanted to hurt them in any way. It was so strange because when you leave the priesthood you're virtually 'disappeared' – there are no leaving parties, only a feeling of ejection and rejection. Years later I told my ordaining bishop, the man who ordained me, what had happened and why I left. He just took my hand and said to me, 'I understand.' It was so pastoral, so beautiful. You see, I've never fallen into the trap of confusing the experience of Jesus with the experience of the Church.

"Will the Catholic Church change its teaching? Not really. The refusal-to-judge statement from Pope Francis was a major moment, but that's as far as we're going to go, I think. Which is sad. I'll tell you what is the elephant in the room and it involves celibacy. If the Roman Catholic Church said tomorrow that priests did not have to be celibate, some of them would marry but a lot of them would not. A lot of them. And that would start to reveal just how many Catholic priests are gay, and I mean cardinals and bishops included, and that terrifies the hierarchy. We need daringly loving words from the Church right now, and while I had no hope for years that we'd hear anything like that, I do now at least have some hope. That's going to have to do for the time being I'm afraid."


I conducted many other interviews, but the ones I have included are a fair representation of the anecdotes and experiences of gay Christians. One person I did not meet was Timothy Kurek but his story is worth a brief mention. In 2009 in Nashville, Tennessee, Kurek, a graduate of the conservative Christian Liberty College and someone who had opposed equal marriage and gay rights for most of his life, pretended to be a gay man for a year and "came out" to his friends and family. He recorded the story in the book *The Cross in the Closet*[2] and was motivated to do all this after a friend told him of how her family had rejected her when she told them she was a lesbian. He doubted her story, even when she cried in his arms, and admitted that he was more interested in what arguments he could use to tell her she was wrong than in helping in a time of anguish. The idea of posing as a gay man is deeply problematic on any number of levels, and some of the gay people who befriended him now feel understandably betrayed. But what Kurek experienced should be a life lesson for those Christians who still believe that the conservative stance against homosexuality is based exclusively on love and a genuine concern for their well-being. "You learned to be very afraid of God in church," says Kurek, "and you learned the loving thing to do is to tell my friend who is gay, 'Hey, listen, you are an abomination and you need to repent to go to heaven.' I absolutely believed in that lock, stock, and barrel." He told most of his friends and family that he was gay, found a job in a gay café, played softball with gay men, and went to gay bars, always remaining a conservative Christian. He found that 95 per cent of his friends stopped talking to him, and his mother wrote in her journal that she'd rather have been told by her doctor that she was dying of cancer than hear that her son was gay. But, he readily admits, none of what he faced comes in any way close to what genuinely gay people experience, especially if they have been raised in conservative Christian homes. He insists that while there may be a great deal of ignorance and fear within conservative Christianity regarding homosexuals, genuine hatred is limited to a vocal minority. And within the shouts of abuse, insults, and rejection there is a song of hope – his mother gradually changed her views and is now an ally of the gay community.

There are countless other stories, of course, and so many more that are yet to be lived and yet to be recorded. God willing they can generally be happier tales with happier conclusions, but that will take work, change, acceptance, and great leaps of love and understanding. We'll discuss what the future might hold in the next chapter.

# THE FUTURE

WHILE THE WESTERN WORLD BECOMES increasingly used to equal marriage and largely comfortable with gay people and realizes that a person's sexuality, whatever it may be, is no indicator of moral standing one way or the other, it is only various Christian churches that stand in opposition and isolation to what is seen by the vast majority of people as progressive, enlightened, and fair. Other religions have different agendas and challenges and their opinions are not really within the purview of this book. Judaism in its reform, liberal, and even sometimes conservative branches is increasingly accepting of equal marriage, and although orthodox Judaism is not, it's a small community and, frankly, those adherents who may be gay or disagree with its teaching tend to leave for a less strict form of the religion. Hindus, Sikhs, Buddhists, and other faiths vary greatly in their approach, and while Islam has not moved on the issue and is hardly likely to in the foreseeable future, it is yet to influence the greater debate one way or the other. As this book is primarily about the Christian approach and why one Christian in particular – the author – changed his opinion, we need to consider at least some of the various Christian denominations, where they stand and where they might change. I'm not going to indulge in a detailed account of individual church teaching because we don't have the room and most people don't have the interest. So, broad strokes, if you'll forgive me, but within those broad strokes we can identify some definite changes and record what has happened and what might be likely to occur. Christianity is not uniform, of course, and we can break it up broadly into Roman Catholic, evangelical, mainstream or perhaps liberal Protestant, and Eastern Orthodox. I'm not going to devote much space to the last of these because so many Orthodox churches are tied closely to their ethnic base and historical circumstances. The largest, the Russian Orthodox Church, has a large diaspora, and within those exiled churches there are some interesting and encouraging discussions taking place about equal marriage and homosexuality, but within Russia itself, the Orthodox Church, linked so closely to the state, is at its most senior and many of its local levels extremely opposed to anything like the rights that gay people enjoy in the West, and the notion of same-sex marriage is outside any theological dialogue at this point. This may change but it will take a very long time. The Orthodox churches of Greece, Bulgaria, Serbia, and others in Europe have a similar approach and the Orthodox churches of the Arab world in particular have, alas, other problems and challenges with which to deal at the moment. The truth is that the entire question of sexuality is much further from the centre of dissent and conversation within Eastern Orthodoxy than in churches with a more substantial Western base, which is inevitable but also regrettable in that this ancient church has so much to offer the world. So for those gay people in the Orthodox Church and those within the Orthodox churches struggling for change, please forgive my omission.

It is undeniable, however, that it is in the Western world and in the Catholic and Protestant churches that the most interesting and encouraging conversations are taking place on issues of sexuality. Several of the more liberal Protestant churches, or at least particular churches within those more liberal denominations, such as the Presbyterian Church (USA), the Evangelical Lutheran Church of America, the United Church of Christ in the United States, the United Church in Canada, and several smaller churches in northern Europe, allow for same-sex marriage, and others provide blessings for gay couples. Many, however, are still divided on the issue or are officially opposed to equal marriage for pragmatic as well as theological reasons. The United Methodist Church is the largest mainline Protestant church in the United States with 12.8 million members, and although it forbids same-sex marriages, there is a growing opposition to Church policy to the extent that ordained United Methodist clergy have actually officiated at gay wedding ceremonies. Perhaps the most significant and interesting church with regard to international consequences and the influence of the wider argument is the Episcopalian Church in the United States, in effect the Anglican Church or Anglican Communion in the United States and thus the branch of Anglicanism in the wealthiest and most powerful nation in the world. While it is smaller in numbers than the Evangelical Lutheran Church with its 3.8 million members, the Episcopalians are part of an Anglican Communion composed of more than 80 million people in dozens of countries in several continents and it is, of course, the state church in England. So Anglicanism has in many ways an influence far greater than its numbers.

In the summer of 2015 in Salt Lake City in Utah, the U.S. Episcopalians voted in the denomination's national assembly to approve religious weddings for same-sex couples, just a few days after the country's Supreme Court had voted in a profoundly important decision to legalize equal marriage nationwide. The motion received a comfortable majority of support in the House of Deputies, composed of clergy and laity, following an earlier vote by the bishops that had supported equal marriage by 129 in favour opposed to a mere 26 against. The Church's website stated at the time, "Rapid changes in civil law concerning marriage in the United States, along with the responses received as part of the SCLM [Standing Commission on Liturgy and Music] church-wide consultation process, indicate a need for equivalent proper liturgies in jurisdictions where same-sex marriage is legal. . . . Further, the consultation process indicated a pastoral need for equivalent marriage rites that could be used by any couple." Thus the decision was not the result of some rushed process or quick decision and occurred only after years of study, prayer, disagreement, and – it must be said – sometimes severe conflict. But as the social climate changed, so did the religious, and by 2015 the result of the vote seemed almost inevitable. In the months since the acceptance of equal marriage by the Episcopalian Church, those more conservative pundits who predicted crisis and division have been proved wrong, and the denomination of almost 2 million people, which has seen a worrying decline in numbers in recent years, has even witnessed a small but active increase in interest and enthusiasm, especially among younger Americans. Bishop Michael Curry of North Carolina, the newly elected presiding bishop and the first African American to lead the church, said powerfully and poignantly that the Supreme Court of the United States "affirmed the authenticity of love" by legalizing gay marriage and that the church had no Christian option but to do the same.

It's sad to say but that authenticity of love is still dividing the Anglican Communion internationally. Back in 2003, Gene Robinson, an openly gay man who was divorced from his wife, was elected bishop of New Hampshire. After the 2015 vote, he argued, "Conservative churches are hemorrhaging young people because young people today have gay, lesbian, bisexual, and transgender friends. In increasing numbers, they do not want to belong to a church that condemns their friends that they know to be wonderful people." He ought to know. Only twelve years ago, however, Robinson was obliged to wear a bulletproof vest during his ordination ceremony as a bishop. The physical threats and level of abuse projected at him by opponents was astounding and sometimes terrifying. Some of the vitriol expressed by those opposed to an openly gay man becoming a bishop was particularly shocking, because while often it was from the hysterical and the basement-dwelling, there were ordained clergy and respected commentators who made the most hideous remarks. For example, Robinson had long supported an organization to help young gay people and that group's website apparently had among its many links some to sites that could be considered pornographic. The degrees of separation between Robinson and the pornographic sites were many and no serious person could reasonably allege knowledge or connection. But the mud was still thrown. David W. Virtue is a long-time opponent of gay rights in the church and equal marriage and he claimed spectacularly that "Gene Robinson's website is linked by one click to 5,000 pornographic websites."[1] It simply wasn't. The problem was that so many wanted, and still want, to believe the rumours that they are still repeated as truth. Virtue, for example, is one of the more busy and vociferous of anti-gay campaigners in the Anglican Communion and he has claimed to have 3 million people reading his website and blog. It may well be true. If so, they read comments such as "Same-sex intercourse cannot offer this gift or lead to generativity or natural birth, but only to fleeting individualistic, narcissistic pleasure that may haunt memory, undermine identity, and sear conscience" and "Never before in church history has the ontology and cosmology of human sexual behavior been so challenged. Not even the Borgia Popes dared challenge the definition of sexuality, however debauched their behavior was."

Preferring brotherhood to Borgia, Robinson himself was astoundingly gracious and forgiving through most of this. He later wrote, "Still, as a straight person, you might say, 'This just isn't my fight.' No, it isn't. Unless you care about the kind of society we have. Unless you want the society of which you are a part to be a just one. Unless you believe that a free society, not to mention a godly religion, should fight injustice wherever it is found. Unless your religion tells you – as our entire Judeo-Christian heritage does – that any society will be judged by the way it treats its most vulnerable. Unless you care about our children. Unless fairness matters to you. Unless violence against lesbian, gay, bisexual, and transgender people concerns you. Unless 'liberty and justice for all' is something you believe applies to all our citizens."[2]

But while there is still dissent and division in the United States, a clear direction is taking form from both leadership and grassroots and at this point there is no going back. In Britain, in Canada, and in much of the Anglican Communion worldwide, the discussions are slow and often painful but at least they are taking place. Part of the problem facing these denominations beyond those within their own domestic churches who oppose equal marriage is that they are justifiably frightened of dividing the world Communion if they themselves accept such a change regarding sexuality and marriage.

The principal reason is that in Africa, in particular, but also the West Indies and elsewhere, the opposition to gay marriage and, it must be admitted, to basic homosexual rights and equality is not only substantial but, at least outside of specific regions such as South Africa, often increasing. In 2014, Archbishop of Canterbury Justin Welby felt obliged to issue a joint statement to the leaders of Anglican churches internationally emphasizing the need to "demonstrate the love of Christ" to same-sex couples. The letter also referred back to an earlier document condemning the "victimization or diminishment of human beings whose affections happen to be ordered towards people of the same sex." It was clearly a response to the homophobia of many African Anglicans and a rebuke to church leaders in that continent who have done little to counter the attacks and sometimes even enabled and legitimized some groaningly anti-gay attitudes. Coming from Archbishop Welby, the statement was stinging in that while he is certainly not someone who would ever be capable of hateful speech, he has maintained a more traditional Christian response to the marriage question. It also came shortly after Nigeria had introduced even harsher laws regarding homosexuality, making homosexual acts punishable with up to fourteen years in prison and ten years even for public acts of gay affection – whatever they may be. Uganda had also recently made its anti-gay laws even tougher. In both countries, numerous Christians leaders have supported the moves and often initiated them. The Anglican Primate of Nigeria, the Most Reverend Nicholas Okoh, has been one of the most shamefully eager public figures condemning homosexuality, frequently quoting Genesis as a warning of the eschatological consequences of a nation or a people accepting gay relationships.

It's all become extremely volatile in Africa, and nobody is showing any indication of backing down. African prelates have threatened to withdraw their priests who are training or working in countries where the Church accepts equal marriage and in some cases have acted on their threats. They have repeatedly condemned homosexuality as being "un-African" and tried to paint it as a product of European colonization of the continent. It's disingenuous at best in that the idea that there was no homosexuality in Africa before Europeans settled is frankly laughable. It's more accurate to say that much of the homophobia and the anti-gay legislation that exists in modern Africa and the Caribbean has origins in the time of European and in particular British colonial rule when London introduced and imposed its laws on black Africa. So rather than homophobia being some perverse form of African pride and a gesture of autonomy and defiance toward the West, it's more part of the moral detritus of empire. But rational argument doesn't always apply in this case. Bishop Peter Akinola, chairman of the Council of Anglican Provinces in Africa, has stated, "You now have men and men co-habiting, which is against the African way of life. The Western world is embroiled in a new religion which we cannot associate ourselves with." The Reverend Joseph Ogola, dean of the Anglican Church in Kisumu, western Kenya, made a more specific and, I suppose, honest point when he argued, "I don't like the idea of gay bishops. It is against the Bible. I accept we live in a changing society and have to accept that people value their own freedom, but that should not be linked to the church. They should branch off and start their own religion." That very possibility of split and secession is a genuine one and it's at the centre of the consideration of Church of England leaders, some of whom may be personally and theologically sympathetic to equal marriage but are understandably terrified of dividing their beloved Anglican Communion if they reform church teaching. Their anxiety is understandable but in the final analysis the truth and morality of the argument must triumph over the possible dangers of division. There are certainly elements of blackmail, guilt, and confused loyalties in all of this, but the constant factor is that the victims are gay men and women. In the West they still face relative exclusion in Anglican churches, and in Africa they live the daily reality of persecution. Even in traditionally more tolerant countries such as Kenya and Tanzania, local and federal legislatures are implementing fierce anti-gay legislation, often with the support of local churches.

It's likely that the centre cannot hold. American Anglicans have made their position clear; the Canadian Church is debating the issue and will continue to do so for the next few years but even now boasts many openly gay clergy and a leadership that is increasingly supportive of equal marriage; Australia and New Zealand are divided, but the conservative wing of the former is strong and aggressive; the Church of England operates in a country with full equal marriage and in a culture that no longer comprehends opposition to complete gay equality. Will Africa change to accept the changes or will the Church of England refuse to change so as to continue the denial? I prefer to ask the questions rather than risk the answers.

To add to the African situation, there are always well-financed groups and individuals in Europe and North America eager to help those African Christians who oppose gay rights. It's a sordid case of imperialism by other means. This comes less from an Anglican than an evangelical base; one of the leading players is Scott Lively, who has been one of the most prominent Christian opponents of gay equality for some years and is still as active and popular as ever. He has many followers in the United States but in the past few years has become a fairly major figure in the African debate. His comments show no sign of restraint and, if anything, he and his followers seem to feel increasingly obliged to be more aggressive and forthright. He has, for example, said that homosexuality and pedophilia "are equated. They are equated because the very same arguments you can make for homosexuality you can apply to pedophilia in many ways, not in every way but in many ways. . . . . Clearly it's not the way it ought to be. It's wrong and it should be discouraged." He also believes that "the gay movement is an evil institution [whose] goal is to defeat the marriage-based society and replace it with a culture of sexual promiscuity in which there's no restrictions on sexual conduct except the principle of mutual choice" and that "we've seen the transformation of America, when at the pinnacle of its Christianity was probably in the 1950s. Ever since then it has been declining, why? Because of the sexual revolution. Where did the sexual revolution come from? The sexual revolution came from the activists of the American gay movement."[3] The truth is that those who are more hardline conservative Christians in North America have lost battle after battle on moral and sexual issues and they have come to realize that the best they can do now on home ground is to fight some sort of withdrawing action and keep the remnant alive and informed. In Africa and the Caribbean, however, they see virgin territory that is open to modern media, Western activism, and, most of all, U.S. money. They explain to their audiences that Christians in Africa and the Caribbean can learn from their mistakes. Instead of working to improve living conditions for the mass of Africans, they have spent their time trying to worsen living conditions for gay Africans. It's difficult to forgive that behaviour.

The Right Reverend Dr. Alan Wilson is the Bishop of Buckingham in the Church of England and in 2014 published *More Perfect Union: Understanding Same-Sex Marriage*. He has also been a good friend and advisor to me through the past two years. Wilson has seen the debates over the issue at the centre of the struggle and he puts it like this:

The divides are about two subjects: first is anthropology – there has been a revolution in the way our science leads us to see ourselves. The result of this is to see all human sexuality as a natural phenomenon that can be measured according to various scales, rather than as a binary essentialist reality. It follows that being gay, as much as being straight, is part of creation rather than an offence against it. A common moral standard applies to all sexuality, rather than the assumption that being gay is inherently disordered. This revolution is as fundamental as those induced by Galileo or Darwin. As with those other revolutions the option is therefore for Christians to argue that the bible teaches the world is a round disk at the centre of the universe, that was created in seven days. Most Christians, however, would regard those revolutions as enriching rather than destroying their Christian worldview. The bad news about this divide is extremely deep. The good news, for the Church anyway, is that it is not a strictly theological divide.

The second is inductive versus deductive theology – some people derive their theology from ideals that they then apply to people, whilst others instinctively begin from the human end and derive their ideals in an emergent way from the processes involved in redeeming the world. The latter approach is not the whole story but it was certainly taken by Jesus on many occasions, for example about big matters of the law like the sabbath. It keys in extraordinarily well with the logic of the incarnation. Such inductive faith will tend to be inclusive. I would resolve the tension between both arguments by reference to Jesus' ways of dealing with the Pharisees, and St Paul's teaching about the law and grace. I would say that in the course of rethinking my position on gay people I have made friends afresh with St Paul![4]

That's a compelling analysis and the sort of thing that some people, at least within evangelical Protestantism, are beginning to grapple with. The evangelical position is in many ways more paradoxical than we think. While evangelical teaching is generally conservative and even reactionary on issues of homosexuality, and some evangelical leaders have intensified their attacks on equal marriage, there is an emerging resistance, especially from younger evangelical Christians. Because evangelicalism does not look to a central human authority and relies instead on the individual conscience formed in faith to take inspiration and instruction from scripture, there is obviously more room to manoeuvre here. And manoeuvre there most certainly has been. Some members of the new generation of evangelicals are increasingly looking to challenges such as environmental protection, economic inequality, and social justice rather than the past generation's often static and enervating – and to their children sometimes baffling – concentration on abortion and homosexuality. This is a generation that has grown up with gay friends, in a gay-friendly climate, and with a familiarity with gay married couples. Contrary to what they had been told, the sky has not fallen, no church has been forced at gunpoint to marry a same-sex couple, and Jesus can still be worshipped. These young people feel it's irrelevant and simply pointless obsessing about an issue that seems to be outside of the dialogue about Christian values and ethics. What so many of them say now is that it just doesn't really matter very much. We need to emphasize that this is certainly not the majority view at the moment within evangelicalism, and because of the strong cultural pulls of the Bible Belt and certain local communities, any lasting change will take much longer. The evangelical community has to a certain extent established an alternative to mainstream society with its own schools, colleges, literature, media, and politics. It's difficult to break out of such an upbringing and self-identity. But the indications are that change is a genuine possibility. On June 8, 2015, for example, the author and pastor Tony Campolo released a statement that sent shockwaves through the evangelical world. Campolo might not have the wide public profile of some Christian leaders such as Jimmy Swaggart, James Dobson, Joyce Meyer, or Rick Warren, but within the Christian world he enjoys enormous respect. He was one of President Bill Clinton's spiritual advisors when the president was experiencing his own marital problems and has been a most eloquent voice on what we might describe as the evangelical left or the progressive evangelical movement for many years. His books are extremely popular, his speeches attract enormous numbers, and some Christians believe he delivered the most important sermon of the last few decades with "It's Friday but Sunday's Coming." Most significant of all in this case is that while Campolo has never been considered a political conservative, he has always enjoyed a certain regard and even partial acceptance among theological conservatives within the evangelical movement, and he has spoken to traditional Pentecostal and Baptist churches that would usually have closed their doors to any Christian leader considered a liberal. Although he has always called for dialogue and compassion on the gay issue, he has retained the conservative position, clearly stating on my own television show in the early 2000s, for example, that "marriage is the union of one man and one woman." That he would change his position so publicly and resolutely stunned many people and will have lasting and positive repercussions. Frankly, it may also have negative consequences on his efforts to raise money for his splendid work in the inner city among the unemployed and the poor and alienate him from many evangelicals. So all this comes at a cost, which any Christian who has embraced equal marriage can tell you and which Campolo doubtless knew. Even so, he did the right and the brave thing in that June 8 statement:

> As a young man I surrendered my life to Jesus and trusted in Him for my salvation, and I have been a staunch evangelical ever since. I rely on the doctrines of the Apostles Creed. I believe the Bible to have been written by men inspired and guided by the Holy Spirit. I place my highest priority on the words of Jesus, emphasizing the 25th chapter of Matthew, where Jesus makes clear that on Judgment Day the defining question will be how each of us responded to those he calls "the least of these". From this foundation I have done my best to preach the Gospel, care for the poor and oppressed, and earnestly motivate others to do the

same. Because of my open concern for social justice, in recent years I have been asked the same question over and over again: Are you ready to fully accept into the Church those gay Christian couples who have made a lifetime commitment to one another? While I have always tried to communicate grace and understanding to people on both sides of the issue, my answer to that question has always been somewhat ambiguous. One reason for that ambiguity was that I felt I could do more good for my gay and lesbian brothers and sisters by serving as a bridge person, encouraging the rest of the Church to reach out in love and truly get to know them. The other reason was that, like so many other Christians, I was deeply uncertain about what was right. It has taken countless hours of prayer, study, conversation and emotional turmoil to bring me to the place where I am finally ready to call for the full acceptance of Christian gay couples into the Church. For me, the most important part of that process was answering a more fundamental question: What is the point of marriage in the first place? For some Christians, in a tradition that traces back to St. Augustine, the sole purpose of marriage is procreation, which obviously negates the legitimacy of same-sex unions. Others of us, however, recognize a more spiritual dimension of marriage, which is of supreme importance. We believe that God intends married partners to help actualize in each other the "fruits of the spirit," which are love, joy, peace, patience, kindness, goodness, faithfulness, gentleness and self-control, often citing the Apostle Paul's comparison of marriage to Christ's sanctifying relationship with the Church. This doesn't mean that unmarried people cannot achieve the highest levels of spiritual actualization – our Savior himself was single, after all – but only that the institution of marriage should always be primarily about spiritual growth.[5]

He went on to explain that he had known so many gay couples over the years who had helped him as a Christian and had been models of Christian marriage that he could not reject their example any longer. As a social scientist, he argued, he believed that sexual orientation was almost never a choice and that the idea of trying to "cure" someone was not only damaging but also un-Christian. He concluded by writing that he had heard all the arguments against equal marriage – as, of course, most of us have time and time again – and understood them but now rejected them.

The reaction was immediate, with allies rejoicing and opponents doing what they do best and attacking Campolo for any number of reasons. It felt all the more threatening to Christian conservatives as it came only a year after the well-known Christian singer Vicky Beeching made in some ways an even more revolutionary choice. Beeching is a homophobe's nightmare. More specifically she is a right-wing, anti-gay Christian's nightmare. Young, beautiful, polite, gifted, eloquent, and once a star of evangelical Christian entertainment, she is never strident, is always reasonable, is delightfully inoffensive, and makes compelling personal, moral, emotional, and theological arguments about the need for full acceptance of openly gay people in the church and for the approval of same-sex relationships and equal marriage. Vicky is gay. I first corresponded with her shortly after a British television program presented her story, and since then she has been a champion of equal marriage and other progressive causes. Until the summer of 2014, however, she was a highly popular gospel singer from an evangelical home in Kent, England, who after studying theology at Oxford University landed a prized EMI recording contract that led her to Nashville as a singer-songwriter. She was in great demand and appeared on many Christian radio and television shows, including the *100 Huntley Street* program in Canada – the most successful Christian show in the country – that a year later banned me from their studio and show because of my support for equal marriage.

She told journalist Patrick Strudwick that when she was a small girl, she read in children's picture books "about the destruction of Sodom and Gomorrah – hailstones of fire raining down on these cities known for the 'abomination' of homosexuality. It was viewed as a terrible evil, the cause of the floods. I don't think that my parents brought it up – it was just a given. . . . Realising that I was attracted to [girls] was a horrible feeling. I was so embarrassed and ashamed. It became more and more of a struggle because I couldn't tell anyone. . . . I increasingly began to feel like I was living behind an invisible wall. The inner secrecy of holding that inside was divorcing me from reality – I was living in my own head. Anybody I was in a friendship with, or anything I was doing in the church, was accompanied by an internal mantra: 'What if they knew?' It felt like all of my relationships were built on this ice that would break if I stepped out on to it." [6] She struggled with her homosexuality; had people pray for her and scream for Satan to let her go and transform her sexual feelings; and resisted so much of what she felt and what she was that she became desperately lonely and in overwhelming pain. She tells her story with such modesty and in such an underplayed, quintessentially British way that it makes it all the more moving. In all honesty, the first time I saw her interviewed I had tears in my eyes, and her experience still moves me very much indeed. Here was someone who only wanted to follow God and do her best for Him. In her peripatetic search for some sort of closure or resolution, she went to California but found herself booked to sing at concerts that were put on by opponents of equal marriage; if they'd discovered that she was gay, the EMI "morality clause" would have led to her immediate dismissal. In her early thirties she developed an auto-immune disease called linear scleroderma morphea and a form of the disease called coup de sabre. It hardens the skin and can corrupt the internal organs and even be fatal. One of its causes is profound stress. After a year and a half of chemotherapy and rest and unable to work or be in any way active, she decided that by the age of thirty-five she had to come out. She has never had a gay relationship and didn't know any openly gay people but was determined to help all those other young Christians who had gone through the hell she had experienced. Many of them, tragically, had never known their thirty-fifth year because they had taken their lives while teenagers.

Since then her bitingly reasonable approach and irresistible story have converted countless people, Christians and otherwise, to a different attitude toward homosexuality. Some of them still reject equal marriage but have tempered their response and vocabulary; others have seen the humanity and the individual person behind the harsh theology they had once maintained and have become advocates for same-sex marriage. They realized through Vicky's example that the God of love is the God of the out gay person and the committed gay couple too. None of this would have been possible just a few years ago and although Tony Campolo and Vicky Beeching are but two people, albeit important people, in the Christian world, they are being followed by dozens of others. Change is coming.

I mentioned Steve Chalke earlier when discussing the Biblical arguments used against equal marriage. He's one of the most high-profile evangelicals in Britain, and in early 2013 he issued an elaborate and considered statement on gay rights and marriage and sent the British Christian world into a liturgical dance of either panic or rejoicing. Chalke is a television personality and for many people the attractive, intelligent, and eminently reasonable public face of evangelical Christianity. He is also highly respected for his work with homeless and troubled young people and for living his faith at a personal and effective level. He placed an extensive defence of gay rights and equal marriage on the website of his charity, the Oasis Trust, but also wrote a briefer account for the British magazine *Christianity*. "I feel both compelled and afraid to write this article. Compelled because, in my understanding, the principles of justice, reconciliation and inclusion sit at the very heart of Jesus' message. Afraid because I recognise the Bible is understood by many to teach that the practice of homosexuality, in any circumstance, is a sin or 'less than God's best'. Some will think that I have strayed from scripture – that I am no longer an evangelical. I have formed my view, however, not out of any disregard for the Bible's authority, but by way of grappling with it and, through prayerful reflection, seeking to take it seriously. . . . It's one thing to be critical of a promiscuous lifestyle – but shouldn't the Church consider nurturing positive models for permanent and monogamous homosexual relationships? Tolerance is not the same as Christ-like love. Christ-like love calls us to go beyond tolerance to want for the other the same respect, freedom and equality one wants for oneself. We should find ways to formally support and encourage those who are in, or wish to enter into, faithful same-sex partnerships, as well as in their wider role as members of Christ's body."[7]

Reactions were swift. The Evangelical Alliance, the umbrella group in the United Kingdom that represents a number of evangelical churches and organizations, immediately suspended the membership of the Oasis Trust. The trust was founded by Chalke in 1985 and now works in eleven countries on five continents. It brings health care, housing, education, and help to people in need but because of the view of its founder on equal marriage it is no longer considered worthy to be included as an evangelical Christian entity. There were other criticisms and attacks, of course, but also a stout defence from Christians who had seen Chalke grappling with this issue within the context of a committed faith for many years. As with most Christians who come to a new insight about sexuality, it was not a rushed decision and was decided after much prayer and – important this – much experience. What we saw through the whole episode was that Steve Chalke won many people over to a new, positive view of Christianity but lost quite a few Christians at the same time and for precisely the same reasons. But there were also Christian voices finally emboldened enough to speak out in defence of Chalke and, more importantly, in defence of what he said. There is no indication that Tony Campolo, Vicky Beeching, and Steve Chalke coordinated their statements and actions but what the three of them did is indicative of a greater trend in evangelical thought and attitudes. Countless Christians are doing the same sort of thing in a less public and high-profile way. Sadly though, and perhaps predictably, the reaction against all this positive change is equally strong. And because conservative Christians feel under attack, they are speaking out more loudly and more firmly than in the past.

Take the case of Franklin Graham, the son of Billy Graham, who was perhaps the most respected evangelical leader of modern times. Billy was renowned for being surprisingly apolitical whenever possible, especially as he aged and matured, even to the chagrin of some of his supporters. Although Billy Graham certainly never made any public comments that would have encouraged supporters of equal marriage, he was generally scrupulous in avoiding the issues that divided or caused controversy within the church. This is not the case with son Franklin. When the U.S. Supreme Court legalized same-sex marriage in 2015, Franklin appeared on radio with the perennially over-wrought conservative broadcaster Sean Hannity. The younger Graham told his eager host, "Of course I'm disappointed, but at the same time, I'm not surprised. Our country has been slipping every year further and further away from the God of the Bible – the foundation that our nation was built on. We're slipping away from that. And I believe that we need to do everything we can to warn people of the consequences of sin. Homosexuality is sin. Same-sex marriage is a sin against God. Now, people who don't believe in God don't care about that, but at the same time, Sean, God is going to judge sinners, so I love them enough to warn them of the consequences of sin. And I want everyone who's listening – I'm not here to throw stones at you because you want to marry someone of the same sex – I just want to warn you, and I do this in love, that God will judge sin. God takes sin very seriously. God cannot tolerate sin in his presence."[8]

Some of his other statements, however, have been more inflammatory. In February 2014, for example, he wrote, "Isn't it sad, though, that America's own morality has fallen so far that on this issue – protecting children from any homosexual agenda or propaganda – Russia's standard is higher than our own? In my opinion, Putin is right on these issues. Obviously, he may be wrong about many things, but he has taken a stand to protect his nation's children from the damaging effects of any gay and lesbian agenda. Our president and his attorney general have turned their backs on God and His standards, and many in the Congress are following the administration's lead. This is shameful."[9] If anybody believes that this doesn't matter, they are wrong. It actually matters very much indeed. It is one thing for a Pat Robertson or a Jerry Falwell to speak this way because we'd hardly notice the forest of craziness for the trees of hyperbole. But Graham is different, whether we like it or not. He is the president and CEO of the Billy Graham Evangelistic Association and of Samaritan's Purse, which operates in a hundred countries and has a revenue of more than $300,000,000. His father, Billy, and to an extent even Franklin have the ear of the nation and its leaders, even of its presidents. Quite clearly there is a reaction to progress and a powerful, even panicked, response to what is seen as a pink wedge within the evangelical church. In the United States and to a lesser extent in other parts of the Western world, this could lead to some profoundly ugly scenes.

In some ways, the obvious darkness, abuse, and bold prejudice are easier to deal with than the more subtle discrimination evinced by Christians who wouldn't dream of throwing around too many crass generalizations. One such incident seems to have occurred at Wheaton College in Illinois, one of the evangelical church's premier and most well-regarded universities. Some years ago I delivered a lecture there about English literature and found the staff to be generous and delightful. What did surprise me was that while Wheaton has built its reputation to a certain extent on its research into and collection of books and papers of G.K. Chesterton, C.S. Lewis, and J.R.R. Tolkien, it also operated until 2003 a strict no-alcohol and no-tobacco policy, yet all three of those writers were extremely heavy smokers and dedicated drinkers. More pertinently and painfully, the college has not changed its policy regarding same-sex relationships; this policy caused public conflict in the winter of 2014.

Julie Rodgers was a popular member of staff who had been hired by the college in mid-2013 as an associate for spiritual care in the chaplain's office. Her hiring caused some ripples in the evangelical world because she was known to be gay but she was a declared celibate and as such satisfied at least some of the theological and moral demands of the evangelical world. Her experience was stellar in that she had mentored inner-city teenagers, had an M.A. in English literature, and was a highly sought after church speaker. Much of her work at Wheaton was with Refuge, a community group at the college established for students with same-sex attractions who, because Wheaton regards homosexuality itself as sinful, needed help in remaining celibate and in either abandoning their sexuality or living with it in a celibate manner. Rodgers spent a decade with an "ex-gay" group called Exodus that has now closed. It not only closed but also issued an apology to the gay community, stating that "Exodus is an institution in the conservative Christian world, but we've ceased to be a living, breathing organism. For quite some time we've been imprisoned in a worldview that's neither honoring toward our fellow human beings, nor biblical." That was quite something in that Exodus had worked for decades to lead gay Christians out of their "sinful" lifestyle. Rodgers now thinks that some of what she said and did may have been foolish and pointless and that the chances of her ever marrying a man are about "as likely as becoming Santa's chief elf." But suddenly in July 2015 Rodgers resigned from the college and wrote, "Though I've been slow to admit it to myself, I've quietly supported same-sex relationships for a while now. When friends have chosen to lay their lives down for their partners, I've celebrated their commitment to one another and supported them as they've lost so many Christian friends they loved." The administration at Wheaton refused to offer any public comments other than a blandly neutral release that said she was resigning her position.[10]

It's difficult to know exactly what happened but while Rodgers is adamant that she remains celibate, she is increasingly critical of conservative Christian attitudes toward the entire subject. "No matter how graciously it's framed, that message tends to contribute to feelings of shame and alienation for gay Christians. It leaves folks feeling like love and acceptance are contingent upon them not-gay-marrying and not-falling-in-gay-love. . . . It's hard to believe we're actually *wanted* in our churches. It's hard to believe the God who loves us actually likes us." Her supporters claim that she was forced out of the college because of her evolving views on equal marriage while her detractors insist she should never have been hired in the first place or even be treated as a Christian. Yet she's hardly a radical, hardly a voice shouting for gay marriage in an evangelical college that teaches otherwise, hardly an actively gay woman insisting that her colleagues accept her lifestyle. If someone this moderate and nuanced feels that she has to resign from a Christian college, there is limited hope for those committed Christians who combine their faith in God with their commitment to a loving marriage. As Rodgers tweeted after her resignation, "I do wonder why LBGT questions are one of the only ones we have to be in total agreement upon to be accepted by many Christian communities." That is a profound and essential point and one I have mentioned more than once in this book. We can believe in and love Christ and still disagree with one another on a small and relatively insignificant aspect of Christian teaching. That, at least, seems the reasonable and, one would think, Christian point of view.

There is less to wonder about but more to annoy when it comes to the Roman Catholic Church, not because I am in any way anti-Catholic but because I spent more than twenty years in the Roman Catholic Church, wrote a best-selling about it, and know how it works on numerous levels. That rock is not as secure as one might think. Catholicism is an entirely different matter from its Christian alternatives precisely because, unlike Protestantism, is does look to a central authority and until and unless the papacy and the magisterium in Rome changes its approach and teaching, the Catholic Church will continue to believe and proclaim as it does about homosexuality and marriage equality. It doesn't matter that so many millions of its followers disagree or are themselves gay and are living in committed relationships or that so many of its clergy are gay and, again, many of them are living in long-term partnerships or, as in many cases, have sexual partners in various places and various times. There certainly was, and to an extent still is, a great deal of optimism about Pope Francis and the idea, perhaps an extension of wishful thinking, that the Catholic Church will soon change its position regarding equal marriage or at least adopt a more progressive stance on issues of sexuality. I wish I could agree. While Pope Francis sometimes appears to be empathetic and compassionate in such areas, as when he made his famous remark in July 2013 that "if a person is gay and seeks God and has good will, who am I to judge?", he needs to be understood in a deeper context. This iconic remark was made while he was flying back from Brazil and in response to questions from reporters about an alleged "gay lobby" in the Vatican. He was almost certainly speaking of one particular priest and quickly added that he and the Catholic Church still believed that homosexual acts were sinful but that it was merely the orientation that was not. That has been standard Catholic teaching for some time. And with friends like that, as we have seen, gay people don't need enemies. The Pope surely knows of the number of gay clergy and, one can only assume, wants them to change their ways and thus be forgiven. It's often forgotten that Francis went on to say, "The catechism of the Catholic Church explains this very well. It says they should not be marginalized because of this but that they must be integrated into society."[11] But he then condemned what he referred to as lobbying by gay people. "The problem is not having this orientation. We must be brothers. The problem is lobbying by this orientation, or lobbies of greedy people, political lobbies, Masonic lobbies, so many lobbies. This is the worse problem." With the greatest of respect, sir, that's a statement of colossal naïveté and a quite staggering audacity. He compares campaigns by gay men and women and their allies for basic equality and civil rights with lobbying by "greedy" people and "Masonic lobbies," whatever they may be; Masonic controversies tend to be the preserve of far-right conspiracy theorists and basement-dwelling lunatics. Perhaps in his native Latin America the Masons are an issue but not in the Western world. That Pope Francis gets away with some of this stuff without censure is stunning and says quite a lot about how anxious people are to see him as less rigid than his predecessors. Because a fraction of the papal statement seemed kind and gentle to a people hurt for so long by the Catholic Church, they touchingly, generously, and perhaps rashly thanked him for it. In the months to come, he repeatedly stated the Catholic Church's opposition to gay equality and at one point compared "gender theory" – Vatican code for anything concerning homosexuality and equal marriage – with the doctrine and behaviour of young Italian fascists in the 1930s and even of the Hitler Youth.[12]

As recently as 2010, before he was pontiff, the then-Archbishop Jorge Mario Bergoglio found himself in direct and fierce conflict with the Argentinian government when he opposed its same-sex marriage legislation. "What is at stake," he said, "is the identity and survival of the family: father, mother, and children. What is at stake are the lives of so many children who are discriminated against in advance, deprived of the human maturation that God wanted to give them with a father and a mother. What is at stake is a direct rejection of God's law, which is also engraved in our hearts. Let's not be naïve: it is not just a political struggle; it is a destructive claim against God's plan. It is not merely a legislative bill (this is only the instrument) but a move by the Father of Lies who seeks to confuse and deceive the children of God."[13] It's difficult to imagine how he could have been more direct and clear in his and the Church's position. He described the bill to introduce same-sex marriage and institute gay adoption as follows: "The bill will be discussed in the Senate after July 13. Look at San Jose, Maria, Child and ask them [to] fervently defend Argentina's family at this time. [Be reminded] what God told his people in a time of great anguish: 'This war is not yours but God's.' May they succor, defend and join God in this war." His comment that gay adoption represented a form of "discrimination against children" even led the Argentinian president Cristina Fernández de Kirchner to respond that the remarks suggested "medieval times and the Inquisition."

When Francis visited the United States in September 2015, he was praised for his warmth and approachability, and liberals in particular applauded his references to climate change, the poor, immigrants, and the dangers of unbridled capitalism. Yet he also implicitly but repeatedly spoke in favour of what he called "the family" and warned of the threat to it and to marriage. He also shocked many by meeting privately with Kim Davis, the county clerk in Rowan, Kentucky, who had broken the law by refusing to grant marriage licences to same-sex couples and was briefly imprisoned. She is a hero to the Christian right and a strident opponent of equal marriage and gay equality. She claims that the Pope hugged her and told her to remain strong. Davis is an especially raw and harsh example of those who oppose same-sex marriage – she's a Protestant fundamentalist rather than a Catholic and one who has been divorced three times. That catechism to which he refers is, however, extremely Catholic and remains central and essential to Catholic teaching. It was published in French in 1992 and in English in 1994 and its position on homosexuality is worth quoting at some length if we are to have any understanding of what to expect in the years to come:

> Homosexuality refers to relations between men or between women who experience an exclusive or predominant sexual attraction toward persons of the same sex. It has taken a great variety of forms through the centuries and in different cultures. Its psychological genesis remains

largely unexplained. Basing itself on Sacred Scripture, which presents homosexual acts as acts of grave depravity, tradition has always declared that "homosexual acts are intrinsically disordered." They are contrary to the natural law. They close the sexual act to the gift of life. They do not proceed from a genuine affective and sexual complementarity. Under no circumstances can they be approved. The number of men and women who have deep-seated homosexual tendencies is not negligible. This inclination, which is objectively disordered, constitutes for most of them a trial. They must be accepted with respect, compassion, and sensitivity. Every sign of unjust discrimination in their regard should be avoided. These persons are called to fulfill God's will in their lives and, if they are Christians, to unite to the sacrifice of the Lord's Cross the difficulties they may encounter from their condition. Homosexual persons are called to chastity. By the virtues of self-mastery that teach them inner freedom, at times by the support of disinterested friendship, by prayer and sacramental grace, they can and should gradually and resolutely approach Christian perfection. Fecundity is a gift, an end of marriage, for conjugal love naturally tends to be fruitful. A child does not come from outside as something added on to the mutual love of the spouses, but springs from the very heart of that mutual giving, as its fruit and fulfillment. So the Church, which is on the side of life, teaches that "it is necessary that each and every marriage act remain ordered per se to the procreation of human life." This particular doctrine, expounded on numerous occasions by the Magisterium, is based on the inseparable connection, established by God, which man on his own initiative may not break, between the unitive significance and the procreative significance which are both inherent to the marriage act.

Called to give life, spouses share in the creative power and fatherhood of God. Married couples should regard it as their proper mission to transmit human life and to educate their children; they should realize that they are thereby cooperating with the love of God the Creator and are, in a certain sense, its interpreters. They will fulfill this duty with a sense of human and Christian responsibility. A particular aspect of this responsibility concerns the regulation of procreation. For just reasons, spouses may wish to space the births of their children. It is their duty to make certain that their desire is not motivated by selfishness but is in conformity with the generosity appropriate to responsible parenthood. Moreover, they should conform their behavior to the objective criteria of morality: When it is a question of harmonizing married love with the responsible transmission of life, the morality of the behavior does not depend on sincere intention and evaluation of motives alone; but it must be determined by objective criteria, criteria drawn from the nature of the person and his acts, criteria that respect the total meaning of mutual self-giving and human procreation in the context of true love; this is possible only if the virtue of married chastity is practiced with sincerity of heart. By safeguarding both these essential aspects, the unitive and the procreative, the conjugal act preserves in its fullness the sense of true mutual love and its orientation toward man's exalted vocation to parenthood.[14]

The application of this teaching may be delivered in a more gentle manner or tone in some diocese and parishes, and various clergy and even bishops might not observe every letter of every law but these are mere cosmetic dressings on a body of belief that cannot change without a colossal dislocation of Catholic theology and philosophy and I can envisage no scenario where that might happen. There are, of course, some brave and defiant voices out there, and we should certainly listen to them. Father Timothy Radcliffe is the former Master of the Dominican Order and was appointed by Pope Francis to be a consultor for the Pontifical Council for Justice and Peace, a position he would not have been given by Pope John Paul II or Benedict XVI. He's a delightful combination of the scholarly and the worldly and has long expressed fascinating and, many Catholics would insist, even heretical views on homosexual love: "We must ask what it means, and how far it is Eucharistic. Certainly it can be generous, vulnerable, tender, mutual and non-violent. So in many ways, I would think that it can be expressive of Christ's self-gift." In a lecture back in 2006 he spoke of "accompanying" homosexuals, by which he meant watching gay-themed movies, reading gay literature, and "listening with them as they listen to the Lord."[15] A touch sentimental perhaps but not only does the man have a heart but he has it in the right place.

Johan Bonny is the bishop of Antwerp in Belgium and a delegate to the 2015 Synod of Bishops on the Family. He has argued that "inside the Church, we must look for a formal recognition of the relational dimension that is also present in many homosexual, lesbian and bisexual couples." In a December 2014 interview he said, "In the same way that in society there exists a diversity of legal frameworks for partners, there must be a diversity of forms of recognition in the Church."[16] Cardinal Walter Kasper from Germany is a senior figure in the Roman

Catholic Church and spoke for many North European Catholics when he commented on the Irish referendum that legalized equal marriage in 2015: "A democratic state has the duty to respect the will of the people; and it seems clear that, if the majority of the people wants such homosexual unions, the state has a duty to recognize such rights." Archbishop Bruno Forte of Chieti-Vasto is an Italian theologian who has argued that the Church needs to "accept and value" homosexual orientation and that gay rights should be protected. The new Archbishop of Berlin, Heiner Koch, has said that "any bond that strengthens and holds people is in my eyes good; that applies also to same-sex relationships" and "to present homosexuality as sin is wounding. . . . I know homosexual pairs that live values such as reliability and responsibility in an exemplary way."[17] Cardinal Godfried Danneels, the former archbishop of Brussels, said in 2013 about various states introducing equal marriage, "I think it's a positive development that states are free to open up civil marriage for gays if they want." These men, and the Catholic Church is of course still dominated by men, are far from alone.

This is all very encouraging but they are only a handful of comments from liberal-minded individuals in a sea of conservative opinion and often hidden agendas. Whenever such brave people do speak out, they always face a powerful and organized hostile reaction. Perhaps a more typical example of the way the Catholic hierarchy deals with dissent occurred in Philadelphia in 2015. Teacher Margie Winters did not have her contract renewed – in effect was fired from her job – as a religious instruction director at Waldron Mercy Academy because she had married her female partner, even though she claims she had told the school board about her marriage when she was originally hired in 2007. She says she was told then that it was fine but that she should not share the information with the parents of children at the school. She claims that she obeyed these instructions even though it was difficult for her and put her under great personal strain. It seems that some parents did manage to find out that she was married to another woman and promptly complained to the archdiocese; they contacted the school, which in turn asked her to resign, and when she refused, her contract was not renewed. There is absolutely no evidence that she was failing at her job or that she was discussing her sexuality in class or trying in any way to influence any of the students to change their views nor was she criticizing Catholic moral teaching. She simply was what she was. The principal, Neil Stetser, was obviously under great pressure and told the media that "to continue as a Catholic school," Waldron Mercy had to comply with Church teaching. The archdiocese has denied trying to influence the decision but Philadelphia's archbishop, Charles Chaput, one of the most conservative bishops in North America, stated, "Schools describing themselves as Catholic take on the responsibility of teaching and witnessing the Catholic faith in a manner true to Catholic belief. There's nothing complicated or controversial in this. It's a simple matter of honesty." He also praised the school board for exhibiting "character and common sense for taking the steps to ensure that the Catholic faith is presented . . . in accord with the teaching of the church. They've shown character and common sense at a moment when both seem to be uncommon." In 2010 when he was archbishop of Denver, Father Chaput had supported the diocese of Boulder when two young children of lesbian parents were refused a place in a local Catholic school. The "sins" of mothers as well as the fathers, it seems, continue to the next generation if not beyond. Chaput said at the time that it was a painful decision and that while the Church doesn't look for reasons to reject children from their schools, Catholic views on homosexuality cannot be taught "if teachers need to worry about wounding the feelings of their students or about alienating students from their parents."[18]

The Philadelphia case is something of a microcosm of the contemporary Catholic dilemma. An admired teacher loses her job because she is in a gay union, her sexuality was almost certainly known to her colleagues and superiors and they were indifferent or supportive, most of the children and their parents were delighted with her work, and it could even be that some of the local clergy were aware of the situation – frankly, how could they not be? But a few conservative activists decided to take action, the official teaching of the Catholic Church was quoted, Church officials knew they could not defend the teacher, and then the local bishop made his views clear. Archbishop Chaput happens to be highly conservative but even a liberal bishop would almost certainly have had to do the same thing. In matters Catholic, minds and jobs as well as hands are tied.

Sometimes the Roman Catholic situation becomes tragic and even macabre. In September 2010 at an open-air Mass in Birmingham, England, Cardinal John Henry Newman was beatified. The event had been long-awaited by those who admire the great man, and many English Catholics had spent years working to make the occasion happen. Newman the intellectual, the convert from Anglicanism, the scholar who was not always comfortable with the Catholic establishment, the aesthete who worked with poor and Irish immigrants on the one hand and patrician Englishmen on the other, personified a specific form of English Catholicism that still appeals to many. So this was the culmination of a long, loving campaign. Thing is, Newman was not only a fine priest and a genuinely gifted theologian but he was also someone who spent much of his adult life in love with a man. He described Ambrose St. John, a fellow convert and Catholic priest, as "my earthly light" and the two of them lived together for thirty-two years. St. John would pack Newman's bags for him, look after him, remind him to take his medicine, and make sure he was fed, warm, and happy. There is no evidence that the relationship was ever sexual but in almost all other ways it was a marriage, and when St. John died in 1875 poor Newman was in a state of emotional turmoil and agony. He wrote, "I have always thought no bereavement was equal to that of a husband's or a wife's, but I feel it difficult to believe that anyone's sorrow can be greater than mine." Newman lived for another fifteen years, and in that time he demanded three times that when he died he must be buried in the same grave as the person he loved so very deeply. Most heterosexual men can point to close male friend- ships but the idea of being buried in the same grave and of living with another man as a secular partner for so very long goes much further than that. The Catholic Church, however, thinks otherwise, or perhaps does not think otherwise but says otherwise. It had Newman's body removed from the joint grave when it became obvious that he was to be made a saint and as a consequence his resting place would be visited by large numbers of people who would want to venerate him and pray. Imagine them being greeted by a joint memorial listing the people in front of them as two men who lived together for more than three decades? He would not, of course, have been the first saint to have been gay nor will he be the last one – I personally know many saintly gay men, some of them priests and some of them Roman Catholic, but God forbid a worshipper should be forced to wonder why the object of their devotion was buried in a grave with a man whom he loved with so much sacrifice and dedication. So Newman's final wishes were ignored and contradicted and his cold remains were moved to an even colder resting place in the Oratory Church in Birmingham where he would be alone.

Reviewing two biographies of Newman by Ian Ker and John Cornwall, Reverand Professor Diarmaid MacCulloch had no doubts about the reality and the iniquity of the situation: "Newmanolators cannot abide the idea that he could have been gay. As conservative Roman Catholics, they can't just accept that homosexuality is one unremarkable and morally neutral variant in human behaviour; and so Newman's enthusiastic biographer, Father Ian Ker, has insisted emphatically on Newman's heterosexuality. Reading Cornwell's account of Newman's emotional life – his passionate friendships with other single men (St John was just the most long-lasting), his tortured opinions about his own sinfulness, his obvious revelling in the homosocial world of early Victorian Oxford – it is difficult to avoid applying to him that useful variant of Ockham's Razor: 'Looks like a duck, quacks like a duck – can it be a duck?' Cornwell, otherwise so clear-sighted, avoids this conclusion, though undoubtedly after careful thought. He bolsters his rejection by reference to the homosocial circle of another Anglican convert to Catholicism, Father Frederick William Faber, a monumentally silly man who was undoubtedly and almost explicitly gay. Cornwell's logic seems to run that because Faber behaved in a certain way and was gay, and Newman did not behave like Faber, ergo it is 'ill-conceived' to consider Newman gay. Not a strong argument. All this matters because Newman's sanctity is tangled up with current politics in the Roman Catholic Church, and not just its woes about sexuality."[19]

The point is that even the dead are being used and abused to bolster an increasingly untenable position by conservatives in the Roman Catholic Church. Nobody is arguing that Newman's romantic attachments diminished his vocation as a Catholic priest or prevented him from being a fine man and an inspiring Christian, so it is especially hurtful that history should be twisted into new shapes so as to justify a lasting prejudice. Newman's grave now remains half-empty, without him who was supposed to be there with his life and death partner and that is so terribly sinful. We also have to wonder how many gay Catholic priests were involved in this elaborate theatre of obfuscation and how many will continue to do so and for how long. Sometimes it resembles an absurd, self-loathing game of religious charades. There have been signs of genuine hope. Cardinal Carlo Martini SJ came extremely close to being elected Pope but was beaten by Pope Benedict XVI. He was a genuine liberal and intellectual, and under his leadership there may, just may, have been room for at least the beginning of a change in Church teaching concerning sexuality but instead the last decade has generally been a time of arch-conservatism. Martini died in 2012, and shortly after his death the *Corriere della Sera* published his last interview in which he stated that the Church was two hundred years out of date. "Our culture has aged, our churches are big and empty and bureaucracy rises up, our rituals and our cassocks are pompous. The Church must admit its mistakes and begin a radical change, starting from the Pope and the bishops. The pedophilia scandals oblige us to take a journey of transformation." But those cassocks are difficult to give up and so much can be hidden beneath them.

Beyond the Roman Catholic Church and in the Christian community in general, there is often a palpable sense of persecution, paranoia, and threat with regard to this issue and we can't consider the future unless we address this. I mentioned in the first chapter the great confectionery scandal, when Christian bakers refusing to bake products for same-sex weddings were sometimes understandably prosecuted on grounds of discrimination. But this is just the – please forgive me – mere icing on the cake, and the clash between right-wing Christians and the gay community and the former group's well-funded sense of outrage are worth exploring a little more deeply. In May 2014, for example, a Belfast court ruled that a young couple that owned a bakery and refused to make a cake decorated with a pro-gay marriage slogan had broken the law. They were given a token fine, have become heroes to social conservatives, and intend to appeal the decision. The ruling may have been unjust because the people ordering the cake had asked for a directly political statement to be placed on it, and surely we have a right to object to such a request whatever our politics, but most of us can see both points of view. The outcome was also inevitable because Northern Ireland has legislation protecting members of any community in the profoundly divided region from being refused service. That was actually what enabled the case to happen. Because legislation has been passed to defend Protestants from Catholic or Catholics from Protestant discrimination, a gay couple had been able to successfully sue a Christian bakery. Religious hatred coming to the rescue of a same-sex couple. There's irony for you. But one wonders if the bakers in question would have had a different response if that dastardly cake did not contain a political message and merely announced the marriage of two people of the same gender. It's a delicate issue – rather like a cake, really – because as much as businesses should not discriminate, there should be some sort of protection for freedom of conscience. Yet there is also an invincible nonsense in all of this. Most of the similar cases that have occurred internationally have involved the refusal of a hotel room to a gay couple, the rejecting of a gay woman wanting to buy a wedding dress for her special day, the denial of photographic services to same-sex couples, and so on. Yet as we mentioned earlier in the book and will discuss again shortly, while those refusing to serve gay customers have so far almost always been Christian, Jesus never even speaks of homosexuality but does strongly condemn divorce. There is no evidence at all these devout bakers, hoteliers, dressmakers, and photographers ever refuse service to heterosexual couples who are divorced or who are living together. In fact, as far as we know, they have never even asked. Which leads one to believe that all of this is about something other than faith and is more likely connected to social convention, lack of comfort, and sheer prejudice. We would, no doubt, be incredulous if a bakery refused service to an interracial couple, for example, and although the parallel is not exact, it certainly feels that way if you're gay. If people genuinely followed Christ, they would surely try to imagine how they would feel being rejected once again after centuries of discrimination and abuse, rather than stand firm on the flimsy foundations of icing and sugar. While many Christians involved in all of this constantly claim that they act only out of love rather than prejudice, that love that keeps presenting itself in cases of homophobia sure seems to take on a bewildering shape.

There is even more hypocrisy if we search a little deeper. The issue of withholding service to gay people and gay couples has suddenly become to some of the people involved a cause of freedom and free speech. But many of these new libertarian zealots have been rather controlling of free speech in the past and were traditionally some of the first to call for censorship of what they considered obscene. They certainly tended to say nothing up to now when their opponents were silenced and certainly did not speak up for gay men and women who for so long were denied basic civil liberties. The truth is that for generations and even to this day to a very large extent, conservative Christians, Catholic as well as evangelical, refuse to recognize and deal with what is not their religiosity but with an intolerance loosely founded on a singular interpretation of that religiosity. The time to do so is long overdue, and we will witness repeated battles over rights and freedoms that really have no relevance any longer to the majority of people. North America and Western Europe have, to their great credit, developed a new, liberal, and loving response to these issues and have grown, matured, and prospered as a result. Christianity and Christians should be opening the door to such change, not be dragged through it screaming and protesting. As for what Jesus would do, the answer is simple: He'd bake the cake and then proceed with preaching the Gospel of love, charity, forgiveness, and joy.

But still we have bakers, and for all I know butchers and candlestick makers, in the United States, Canada, and continental Europe behaving in this same way, along with their comrades-in-arms in restaurants refusing to cater same-sex weddings and all the rest of them standing firm on their Christian principles. Good Lord, they're being asked to sell a product, not to sleep with the wedding couple! Nobody has to support equal marriage, and only an extremist would argue that providing what is a necessary but non-essential or religious product for the wedding reception indicates enthusiasm or consent. This is not, for example, anything like a minister or priest being forced to officiate – that has never happened and could never happen and any suggestion otherwise is pure hysteria. But then hysteria is a key factor in all this, accompanied by fundraising activities for the alleged victims that can be extremely lucrative. Be very suspicious of some of these stories of alleged martyrdom. The image of innocent people being forced into bankruptcy or unemployment just because they wouldn't pipe "Mister and Mister" on a wedding cake is not always authentic and sometimes entirely apocryphal. In Oregon, the bakers Aaron and Melissa Klein were fined $135,000 by the courts after they repeatedly refused to serve a lesbian couple who wanted a cake for their wedding. They were being pretty bloody-minded about the thing and were given several chances to move on. But they didn't and have now raised close to $400,000 from churches and support groups. That's a profit of more than a quarter of a million dollars for one cake. Not bad. At all. So "Sweet Cakes by Melissa" seems to be doing rather well and it's not alone. Whenever this happens, and it's extremely rare in spite of what we're told, public funding campaigns, often with the backing of evangelical ministers with mega-churches, raise small fortunes. The refusal to provide services and to break the law also tends to make those suburban rebels heroes to entire communities and leads to any amount of publicity, speaking engagements, and the like. While people have a sacred right to their opinions, other people have a right to be served without bigotry. The same would apply if a conservative Christian was told by a gay caterer or dressmaker that they were not willing to provide services because they objected to their beliefs. This is not about the Bible and its comments on adultery, dishonesty, greed, polygamy, war, and anything and everything else but about a cult of objecting to equal marriages that at heart has nothing to do with the individual consciences of individual Christians.

As for those marriage commissioners who have found their jobs challenged when they have refused to marry same-sex couples, reality cries out to be heard. They are civil servants, bureaucrats, and agents of the civil and secular state, and their job is to administer the law. In many ways they are an alternative or even a counter to organized religion in that they arrange marriages outside and beyond the church. When they marry two people, they do not administer sacraments, do not speak of religion, and include no Christian content in their actions. That these people should suddenly decide that the Christian faith is an intrinsic part of what they do and that because of this they cannot marry same-sex couples is truly astounding. If they cannot do their job, they have to find another one. That's not harsh but fair. That Christian groups have supported and funded marriage clerks in their campaigns as they fight against the law is not only wrong but also baffling in that many of those fighting such cases simultaneously believe in the iron separation of church and state. But then as we have seen so often, consistency of argument doesn't always apply when it comes to opposing equal marriage.

The clash between church and state over equal marriage takes on various forms and will continue to do so in the years to come. In Canada in the past two years, an evangelical university in British Columbia, Trinity Western, has faced difficulties because it plans to open a law school but also insists that students accept what is called a Community Covenant. It's a fairly extensive document, speaks of Biblical principles, and outlines specific but sometimes entirely admirable if intrusive ways of life for students. It does, however, spend an inordinate amount of time dealing with issues of sexuality and, while careful not to name homosexuality, is obvious in its direction. There are at least three references that support that idea. The first says that students must "observe modesty, purity and appropriate intimacy in all relationships, reserve sexual expressions of intimacy for marriage, and within marriage take every reasonable step to resolve conflict and avoid divorce"; the second that members abstain from "sexual intimacy that violates the sacredness of marriage between a man and a woman"; and the third that, "according to the Bible, sexual intimacy is reserved for marriage between one man and one woman, and within that marriage bond it is God's intention that it be enjoyed as a means for marital intimacy and procreation." Errors or generalizations in Bible-reading aside, the reference to divorce is significant in that, as I mentioned earlier in this chapter and in an earlier part of the book, while Jesus never even mentions homosexuality, He stresses that divorce is unacceptable – and this in a Roman, Greek, and Jewish culture that readily accepted divorce as a social reality and sometimes human necessity. So while Trinity Western – and for that matter pretty much every other evangelical university that has a similar code – requests "reasonable" steps to avoid divorce, it does not forbid it and divorce would be no barrier to enrollment. The covenant also, by the way, prohibits "the use or possession of alcohol on campus, or at any TWU sponsored event, and the use of tobacco on campus or at any TWU sponsored event," which is interesting in that tobacco is obviously not mentioned in any Bible I have read. Be that as it may, here we had a Christian college anxious to train lawyers who had to be accredited with various Canadian law societies who not only would have been educated in a restricted, gay-free environment but – and this surely is the damning point – are supposed to be committed to upholding a legal code that not only allows for equal marriage but also holds dis-crimination against gay people to be illegal. Thus the school's covenant arguably breaks the very law it intends to teach in that it denies gay people the freedom to enroll in a specific col-lege as openly gay men and women. So far some law societies have stated they will refuse to acknowledge and accept Trinity Western law school graduates while others have agreed to accept them or are still debating the issue. This seems to be a legal and religious bridge too far even for those conservative Christians who are convinced the world has to adapt to and for them rather than that they work out a reasonable compromise to accommodate modernity.

So where do the rights of conservative Christians and the freedoms of gay people meet and who is to decide? It's a multi-layered and complex issue, and this book is not the venue to fully discuss the subject but, as we have seen, there are waves of double standard, inconsistency, and even hypocrisy here, and it's genuinely difficult to take some Christian statements seriously when we see how selective they are in applying what they see as Biblical principles. A diverse and civilized society has to allow for minority opinion and dissent, even if it does have trembling foundations and even if those very people asking for protection had never given it to those they now claim are attacking them, and even perhaps if they initiated the persecution in the past of those same people. But public and private are different entities. The law, for example, is a public vehicle and a communal tool for administering justice and that justice must be for all. In the case of Trinity Western and the various other Christian laws schools, no evangelical Christian is prevented from attending any law school, even one with many gay students and faculty, but gay people who live openly in same-sex relationships are prevented from attending evangelical law colleges. Most of this will sort itself out as chronology swamps ideology but the new and horribly misplaced persecution complex of a minority of conservative Christians regarding the gay issue has to be exposed for what it is if we are to advance.

A typical example of this paranoia and misleading reporting appeared in an online conservative religious and political magazine called *The Stream* in August 2015. It gave its loyal readers the headline "Bishop Faces Three Years in Jail for Defending Marriage" and then, as is so often the case, other on-line blogs and sites repeated the story and it began to be regarded as common knowledge. It was extremely worrying stuff, whatever one's point of view on the marriage issue. Freedom of opinion and expression is fundamental yet here, once again, we were being told that opponents of equal marriage were being threatened with prosecution and incarceration. Deacon Keith Fournier wrote in the article in *The Stream*, "For using a verse from Leviticus as evidence for the Bible's opposition to same-sex relationships, Bishop Vitus Huonder found himself charged with a hate crime by a group called 'Pink Cross'. In the politically charged language of the present, Bishop Vitus Huonder is a 'conservative' if not an 'extremist.' In fact, he is simply a faithful Catholic Christian. And for that he's being threatened with three years in jail. It's happening in Switzerland, but the conflict epitomizes a wider phenomenon of anti-Christian secularists on both sides of the Atlantic using the courts to target Christians for simply standing up for biblical truth."

But as we read further – if indeed people do read further – we find out that the story, just as with most of these reports that make similar claims, is not at all what it seems. In 2011 Bishop Huonder gave his backing to those parents who wanted to opt out of school sex education because the schools were teaching that same-sex attraction was entirely normal. In 2013 he published a pastoral letter criticizing the gay community and two years later he called for a Swiss priest who had blessed a gay union to be fired. The man's name is obviously legion when it comes to challenging gay people and gay marriage. Pink Cross have asked that he be charged under Article 259 of the Swiss Penal Code, which is a form of hate crime. If he is charged, if he is convicted, and if he receives the harshest and unprecedented penalty, he could, in theory, go to prison for three years. The truth, however, is that this simply could not and would not happen. No priest or minister has been or will be arrested or imprisoned for refusing to marry a same-sex couple. The most critical and even immoderate language is still used by numerous Christians to object to gay relationships. Yet as someone from Canada who travels extensively in the United States, I have been asked many times about those ministers and priests in my country who have been fired and arrested for opposing gay marriage. It's simply not the case! Actually in the Swiss example what Pink Cross said about the priest was that he was entitled to use scripture to oppose equal marriage, "but then he said the words should be applied to real life, which is the equivalent of calling for the death penalty for gay people. We were worried about that. He is the leader of a big church, and he was calling for people to follow his words, and we thought this could be dangerous." A very different story from what the headline had suggested.

No priest or minister has been or will be arrested or imprisoned for refusing to marry a same-sex couple. The most critical and even immoderate language is still used by numerous Christians to object to gay relationships, and if their words lead to violence, legal consequences could follow. We must remember, though, that this is the law for all people, and if gay leaders called for Christians to be attacked, they would face the same response. Yet as someone from Canada who travels extensively in the United States, I have been asked many times about those ministers and priests in my country who have been fired and arrested for opposing gay marriage. Sorry guys, it's a myth. No priest or minister has been fired or arrested in Canada for speaking out against equal marriage. The dark hysteria of right-wing talk radio and conservative Christian sound bites so infects the narrative that what is fantastic becomes accepted wisdom.

Whether we like it or not, the persecution complex will continue in the short term until the novelty fades away and a new generation of people who are mostly sensible on the marriage issue fills the ranks of service providers and even Christian churches. It's mostly a fashion blip in the world of Christian media and has no greater meaning. No conservative Christian will be thrown to the lions. Some churches will continue to discriminate, many gay people will continue to suffer, equal marriage will continue to expand and become accepted and mainstream and even rather boring for all but those directly involved. The shame is that the churches that refuse to widen their Christian love will continue to lose younger people and within a generation or two may well appear as museum pieces. I remember the first time we took our children to a British medieval castle with its requisite dungeon and instruments of torture. "Dad, Mum, did they really used to do that to people in the olden days?" they asked, part incredulity and, truth be told, part hopeful titillation. Yes, kids, they did. And then on to the gift store, some ice cream, and the civilized, modern age in which the kids actually lived. They might even have asked for a slice of cake, and I don't think they would have cared one bit who made it and who else they made it for as long as it tasted good. The thing about the future is that it becomes the present much more quickly than you think and usually with much less pain than you feared.

# LAST WORDS

THERE REALLY IS SO MUCH that can be said about all of this in a final chapter, and it's difficult to know what to include and what to omit. The Church of England priest Canon Mark Oakley has spoken and written eloquently on being gay and being Christian; in one of his first public speeches about his sexuality he spoke in gentle and gracious tones, explaining, "As a boy I was made to feel unloved and unlovable and the experience of gay and lesbian people is such an experience in the playground and at home. We are made to feel shameful. Shame is not guilt. Guilt is 'I have done something wrong.' Shame is 'I am something wrong.' As a priest I was often told that people supported me privately but that I should be quiet about my sexuality, to not wave a flag. The overall effect of self-censorship is self-loathing. And I am sure as I look back that my draw to the Gospel of Jesus Christ at the age of about twelve was that I saw there a glimpse that I might still be loveable after all, that the voice I was hearing from above was different from that which I was hearing on the ground." He goes on to say, "God can bless a battleship or a pet hamster but not two people who love one another." That's such a poignant set of observations. Shame is different from guilt. We all feel guilty at various times but can deal with that guilt and usually quickly forget it. Shame, however, is not the same. As Oakley says, it is the feeling not that one's actions but one's very being is flawed. That is something that cannot be easily dealt with and perhaps never forgotten. To know that some people feel that they are beyond being loved is something that no Christian can ignore, and we can no longer respond with clichés and tired phrases no matter how heartfelt and sincere they may be.

As a straight man, I feel in some ways unqualified but as a Christian man I feel not only qualified but positively obliged to speak out on this issue. I have outlined arguments in the Bible for and against equal marriage; interviewed gay Christians on the matter; and speculated on the future of the relationship between equal marriage and Christianity. But what of the more sweeping arguments against same-sex marriage both from Christian and secular sources, and how are they being used to prevent equal marriage where it is not yet legalized and to tarnish the institution where it is now accepted?

Let me be direct. There really aren't any compelling non-religious arguments against marriage equality. I appreciate that this sounds triumphalist and dismissive, but I've read and heard too many of the protests against the proposition to take any of them very seriously any longer. Frankly I have become impatient. There are no new arguments, only rehashed old ones; there are no new polemics, only louder ones. They still, though, require a response. A quick and brief response, however, in that they fall more into the area of general anti-gay attacks than within the debate on equal marriage. I will give them the space they deserve and, anyway, know that there are entire monographs written in response to all the old regulars.

One of the most common accusations that we hear is that gay marriage is unnatural. This argument is used by the casual bigot as well as the more considered person who tries to couch the word in more philosophical or politically neutral terms: "I'm not being nasty, I just mean that some things are natural and others are not." Whatever their motivation and intent – and I'm far from convinced that they are neutral when they make such comments – equal marriage is not unnatural. It's non-traditional and that's something entirely different. "God created Adam and Eve," we've heard myriad times, "not Adam and Steve." After the U.S. Supreme Court legalized equal marriage in 2015, one wit wrote that he so terribly hoped that the first gay couple to be married after the ruling were actually named Adam and Steve. Alas they weren't, but we can pretend so for the sake of irony. The natural-law aspect of heterosexual marriage is obviously pertinent in that quite clearly men and women have physical complementarities and can procreate, but this assumes that having children is the central purpose of marriage. It also places a major emphasis on sex, and although sex is certainly an important part of marriage, it is not the most significant or even defining one. It could well be argued that marriages demonstrate their strength and commitment after decades of partnership, at an age when sexual activity is at its lowest and may even be non-existent. Marriage is about much, much more than sex. It is bewildering that many of the loudest critics of equal marriage are on the one hand sexual puritans who want to limit sexual activity and seem viscerally and theologically offended by its joy and harmless fun but on the other argue that unless two people can indulge in an act of intercourse that produces a baby their relationship cannot be labelled as a real marriage. Frankly, sex is easy; nursing a spouse through pain and anguish is not. Instantly arousing and physically pleasurable sex is easy; sacrificing and suffering for a spouse is not. If we're going to use the procreative aspect of sex as the only criterion for a natural marriage, it could be argued that sex is "unnatural" when it takes place between a man and a woman who can no longer procreate – perhaps all heterosexual marriages should be considered invalid after the woman reaches an age at which she can no longer conceive. Then there are those married couples who cannot conceive – in such cases they may use in vitro fertilization in an attempt to have children, a process that is hardly natural if we are to use the same strict litmus test thrown at same-sex couples. To be fair, many of the Catholic critics of equal marriage do indeed regard in vitro as unnatural and immoral. There are also people who simply do not want to have children and have a far more negative attitude toward the traditional family than many same-sex couples who work so hard to adopt and raise children, often children abandoned by heterosexual women or straight couples who cannot or will not parent them. Is that natural? Of course mothers and fathers are vital, but the issue is not their gender but the degree of love and devotion they are prepared to give their sons and daughters. Children need parents and all the evidence indicates that children don't care whether their parents are gay or straight but they certainly know if they're good or bad. The reality of the process is that while same-sex couples sometimes arrange for surrogates to have children for them or already have children from earlier heterosexual relationships, they frequently raise children who have no family because heterosexual people have been unable to raise them or have simply rejected them. Gay adoption is part of the entirely laudable campaign to try to repair the outcome of heterosexual sex that, for whatever reason, leads to parentless children. I do not judge those who for whatever reason cannot raise their children but I will judge gay couples who adopt them and judge them to be heroic and loving people who are anxious to give their love to vulnerable children. These are young people, sometimes with challenges and difficulties, who would otherwise be raised in a communal setting that is hardly, here's that word again, natural.

An extension of all this is that equal marriage must be wrong because homosexuality is not found in the animal kingdom and is thus "unnatural." That's a bit of a stretch intellectually and morally but also just plain inaccurate in that animals are indeed sometimes attracted to creatures of the same gender. Ask farmers about gay animals and they'll happily give you stories. But whatever the facts, if we are to base our opinion of human love and the nature of marriage on the activities of dogs, cats, and, for all I know, mice, we're in for a whole zoo of trouble.

The argument continues that the human body is made for a woman and a man to link in sexual union. Yes, we certainly are made that way physically, as long as everything works out healthily. We're also made to walk rather than fly, to run rather than travel under water, and we're even made to fight and even to kill. What the human body *can* do is not necessarily what it *should* do or *has* to do. This argument is always somewhat perplexing coming from Christians in that Christ taught us to work against our natures in a variety of ways such as by embracing our oppressors, turning the other cheek, and losing our lives to find them. Self-preservation is natural, losing the self to gain eternal life is not. I suppose it is unnatural to use machines to destroy cancer or to put one person's heart into another person's body but we certainly do so and applaud those who have made it possible and who perform such procedures. Of course, some Christians oppose transplants, blood transfusions, and life-saving surgery but we will never accept their extreme and bizarre interpretation of the scriptures as being normative, and the vast majority of Christians would resist any attempt to make any such ideology the law of the land. By the way, those Christians who do reject modern medicine also reject equal marriage and believe homosexuality to be terribly sinful.

We are told that gay parents simply can't do the job properly. Actually, it's not fact at all – there is no evidence that gay parents are any worse than their straight counterparts, and the handful of surveys that have taken place are generally tendentious and self-fulfilling. Gay parents have to undergo the same examinations and face the same criteria as straight parents when they apply to adopt and, if anything, have to show more evidence of stability and competence and to work harder as mothers or fathers. Children need good role models but the number of single-parent families today is so high that countless children will never know a father or even who their father is. That doesn't in any way guarantee a damaged childhood – some of the best-formed and most emotionally healthy children I have met have been products of single-parent families – but if the presence of a mother and a father is the criterion for a natural or authentic family, we have to assume that single-parent families are not quite the real deal. In some heterosexual families, fathers are seldom present because of the many hours they work away from the home, and increasingly mothers are working similarly long hours. In many of these heterosexual families, children are in daycare centres or are largely raised by nannies or by their grandparents or are subject to any number of modern permutations – none of these varieties makes the families unnatural or harms the children involved. There was an era when mainstream society and mainstream Christian society in particular viewed these alternatives as deeply troubling, but no longer. People realized through experience that they were worrying about nothing, and they will eventually do so again. Historically, children have often been raised in families that have little resemblance to what we have regarded only for around a century as the "normal" family. No harm was done.

The American Academy of Child & Adolescent Psychiatry wrote in 2013 that "current research shows that children with gay and lesbian parents do not differ from children with heterosexual parents in their emotional development or in their relationships with peers and adults" and are "not more likely than children of heterosexual parents to develop emotional or behavioral problems." Eleven years earlier, the American Academy of Pediatrics had stated, "A growing body of scientific literature demonstrates that children who grow up with one or two gay and/or lesbian parents fare as well in emotional, cognitive, social, and sexual functioning as do children whose parents are heterosexual" and have reiterated that belief several times since. The American Psychological Association, the Child Welfare League of America, and various other respected groups in North America and Europe have all made the same types of conclusions. In a report in 2012, *Live Science*, a highly respected on-line magazine covering the latest developments in science, health, and technology, stated, "Research on families headed by gays and lesbians doesn't back up these dire assertions. In fact, in some ways, gay parents may bring talents to the table that straight parents don't. And while research indicates that kids of gay parents show few differences in achievement, mental health, social functioning and other measures, these kids may have the advantage of open-mindedness, tolerance and role models for equitable relationships, according to some research. Not only that, but gays and lesbians are likely to provide homes for difficult-to-place children in the foster system, studies show."[1]

Inevitably, several attempts have been undertaken to show that gay parenting doesn't work or is inferior to straight parenting but these efforts have either been tendentious or, as even their authors generally acknowledge, extremely partial. But while genuine researchers may admit that their findings are based on too small a sampling or from too short a period to have any significant importance, there are activists who will try to use any material that comes to hand to try to prove their case. Probably the most high profile of these was that by University of Texas sociologist Mark Regnerus, whose findings appeared to prove nuanced but noticeable deficiencies in same-sex parenting. Yet even Regnerus himself admitted after his work began to be exploited by anti-gay groups that its findings didn't prove anything and couldn't be reliably used as an argument for or against equal marriage. What was not always so well publicized was that the study was financially supported by various conservative Christian groups with total contributions of around $1 million and that the University of Texas's College of Liberal Arts and Department of Sociology has since distanced itself from the paper and its findings.[2]

These are excuses rather than arguments and increasingly more desperate devices to attack gay families, gay marriages, and gay parenting. They may sting, but some of the weapons used against equal marriage are positively pernicious. It is wrong, we are told, because gay men molest children in far greater numbers than do straight men. This is a particularly odious smear, and it's bitterly ironic when expressed by conservative Christians in light of revelations about so many members of the Roman Catholic clergy and how the Catholic Church did so little to protect the victims and punish the perpetrators. Conservative politicians, broadcasters, and clerics have made these claims, and in some quarters they have taken on the sorry stature of accepted wisdom. Yet according to the American Psychological Association, "Homosexual men are not more likely to sexually abuse children than heterosexual men are," and the genuine research into this sorry area shows that when men do abuse boys – often very young children – they are looking for any victim rather than a male victim; they are also usually not at all interested in having sexual contact with adult men. The Child Molestation Research & Prevention Institute has concluded that 90 per cent of child molesters abuse children in their own families or in the families of their friends and that around three-quarters of the abusers are in straight marriages and have no history of gay relationships. Those members of the Roman Catholic clergy who abused young people overwhelmingly took advantage of boys but this was primarily because there were no altar girls and, at the risk of sounding crude, boys were more available. Most of the priests convicted were not homosexual and did not have a history of gay relationships. It would be helpful to remember that some of those same-sex couples who now adopt children are raising boys and girls who have been victims of abuse in heterosexual families.[3]

A linked argument is that gay people were themselves sexually abused when they were children and this not only led to them being gay but means that they are damaged as people, unqualified to be parents, and more likely to abuse others. NARTH or the National Association for Research & Therapy of Homosexuality, for example, produced a fact sheet in which it argued, "Although sexual abuse does not directly cause same sex attraction, studies report male sexual abuse of lesbians as generally being twice as high as of heterosexual women, that is, on average, 50 percent of lesbian women report a history of sexual abuse. If family relational dynamics and gender non-conformity are already in place, sexual abuse can clench [sic] the direction of detachment, gender insecurity, and disidentification possibly leading to same sex attraction. . . . Sexual abuse can be emotional, verbal, or physical. A girl who is sexually objectified through inappropriate sexual comments, denied age appropriate privacy or whose father has voyeuristic tendencies, has been sexually violated without ever being touched." This, however, is mild compared to some of the accusations made in some Christian circles about the origins of same-sex attraction. Joseph Nicolosi is one of the founders of NARTH and has become notorious for what is known as reparative therapy and the attempt to "convert" gay people to heterosexuality. He has said that "if you traumatize a child in a particular way, you will create a homosexual condition." [4] Once again, there is no scientific or sociological evidence for any of this.

It's extraordinary how many reasons, some of them contradictory, the Christian right and the anti-gay movement have come up with over the years as they try to explain gay people: strong mother, weak father, absent father, too many sisters, too many brothers, mother too close and loving, peer pressure, and now sexual abuse. It seems that pretty much any family structure or experience will, in the eyes of those who are so obsessed with objecting to homosexuality, produce gay people. What they do not address – because it demolishes most of their arguments – is how families will produce one gay person from several siblings, all of them raised in the identical way and in loving and stable homes; or how one member of a set of twins will be gay and one straight. Also, as with most cases of the reporting of abuse, not all the testimonies are reliable, and it is those who have had abnormal rather than those who have entirely normal upbringings who tend to come forward and identify themselves. That some of them will be gay should come as no surprise because some of the general population is gay. The vast majority of those poor souls who are raised in troubled, unbalanced, loveless, or abusive families are hetero-sexual and have always been and will always be so and no amount of inverted statistics based on a preconceived idea will prove otherwise.

At the root of it all, however, is the belief that is essential to conservative Christians: that nobody is born gay. This is more important than you might think when it comes to the Christian approach to sexuality. If people are born gay, it is an act of nature; if it's an act of nature, it's an act of God; if God creates gay people, they are products of God's will; and if they're products of God's will, no Christian can deny them full equality. It would be like denying equality to black people or women. It would be a denial of God. So Christian opponents of equal marriage are passionate in denying that homosexual-ity is genetic or a product of natural circumstances rather than upbringing or community. The truth is that we don't know if people are born gay or not, and to most of us it doesn't matter very much. The study of cadavers that indicated the possibility of some form of gay gene was far too small to be reliable and told us little. It's intriguing to speculate on what would happen if such a gene were discovered and could be indicated before birth. One wonders what the passionately anti-abortion Christian opponents of equal marriage would say about the inevitable mass abortion of gay unborn children, largely due to a still thriving homophobia partly sustained by those very conserva-tive Christians. The entire gay-at-birth debate is mostly a digression and distracts from the reality that sexuality is no more an indication of worth, morality, or goodness than is being black or white.

Most gay people do not remember a time when they were not gay and when they were not attracted to people of the same gender. Whether they were born gay or not they don't know and wouldn't have the arrogance to claim to know, but most of them do know they have never been straight. There are certainly people who have left heterosexuality or even straight marriages to live as gay people, but if we look at these cases in any depth, it soon becomes obvious that the lie they were living due to family pressure, shame, social disdain, religion, or any number of factors was that they were not gay in the first place. Many have left marriages, often but not always with consequent pain for all concerned, because society had forced them into a false life due to its homophobia. They were gay then and always will be gay. While attitudes have changed dramatically in recent years and societies in the West are far more tolerant than they were, it is still a challenge to be gay. Conditions were exponentially worse in years past though, and thousands of men were arrested and imprisoned for their sexuality as late as the 1960s in a number of advanced nations. The suggestion that people would have chosen to be gay and risk being ostracized, unemployed, assaulted, hated, abused, arrested, and incarcerated is not a very serious one.

So if gays are not abusive, aren't the products of abuse, aren't bad parents, and are probably born gay, toss in the old promiscuity label. Gays and gay men in particular cannot be married and cannot be parents because, we are told, they are so free with their affections. Pride parade nudity, sweaty dancing in dark clubs, and more partners than a Dickensian legal firm.

It's up to gay men and women themselves to decide what they want in their lives, and those gay people who want to be married are obviously interested in stable, committed, long-term partnerships. These partnerships might not always last, of course, which would make them just like stable, committed, long-term, straight relationships. If there is promiscuity among a subsection of gay men, surely the response is not to further marginalize gay people but to include them in the ideal of committed and faithful marriage. On the one hand, opponents of equal marriage condemn gay men for having casual sex, but on the other, they oppose any measure that would involve gay men in a faithful marriage. Having said this, the idea that promiscuity and loveless sexual encounters are the preserve of the gay community is a bit rich when in the summer of 2015 the adulterers' website Ashley Madison was hacked and more than 40 million names made public. The site catered to people in marriages and long-term partnerships who wanted to betray their spouses. One of those publicly shamed was the American Christian television personality Josh Duggar, who was an active opponent of equal marriage and a leading spokesman for the conservative Christian lobbying group the Family Research Council. Spend any Friday or Saturday evening in any city centre in any major Western town and the rowdy, often drunken and loud sexual encounters you will see will, I assure you, be rumbustiously heterosexual. Billions of dollars are spent every year to create environments, venues, and lifestyles for straight people who want to behave promiscuously; the vast majority of pornography is made for straight and not gay people.

With regard to general health, some sub-groups of gay men do sometimes smoke, drink, and use drugs to a greater extent than their straight counterparts but the studies that have shown this – from reliable gay-friendly sources such as Stonewall in the U.K. who admit there are some genuine issues that have to be faced – generally concern younger gay men who are part of the "scene" and not those in stable and long-term relationships. The numbers we have from the limited data available show that men and women in long-term same-sex partnerships and especially marriages have the same or lower use of drugs, tobacco, and alcohol as their heterosexual counterparts and sometimes are more health and lifestyle-conscious.

Then we get back to the quasi-Biblical, with lots of talk about sodomy and sodomites. In my experience, this sort of language is becoming more and not less common in some Christian circles, and it's shocking how for some critics of equal marriage this single act of sex defines gay people. First, it's obviously impossible for women to perform so that reduces it to a potential 50 per cent of the gay community. Out of that 50 per cent, the number of men who engage in anal sex is not as high as you might think. The general figure is regarded as being between 34 per cent and 36 per cent, meaning that around 17 per cent of gay people engage in the act.[5] Yet researchers for a report called "Sexual Behavior, Sexual Attraction and Sexual Identity" in the United States interviewed thousands of people aged between 15 and 44 between 2006 and 2008 and found that 44 per cent of straight men and 36 per cent of straight women admitted to having had anal sex at least once in their lives. Even if we lower the average to 30 per cent, that is a third of a straight population, a population that forms around 95 per cent of the total. These figures may be coldly clinical but what becomes obvious is that a lot more straight people are engaged in anal sex than are gay people. This honestly is a subject unworthy of a grand debate about the future of marriage but it's unavoidable. If one's criteria for rejecting equal marriage and gay rights is the potential health risk of anal intercourse or the fact that it cannot lead to conception, the argument is intellectual bottom feeding. I do apologize. This strange obsession was hilariously if chillingly exposed by the author, actor, and broadcaster Stephen Fry in 2013 in a compelling two-part television documentary entitled *Out There*. It explored the lives of gay people in Brazil, India, Russia, the United States, and Uganda. In the latter, Fry bravely and wittily interviewed a leading Kampala pastor who was part of the homophobic campaign to further criminalize gay sex and even execute people for being homosexual. The encounter took place in a radio studio and began with two men looking at a full-page story in a local tabloid that announced in a headline, "How Bum-Shafting Shattered My Whooper." That pretty much set the tone for the entire debate, with the minister seemingly obsessed with anuses and penises and the most graphic and absurd images of scatological and surgical catastrophes due to gay sex. Fry was incredulous and explained that he was interested in the men he fell in love with and not with their anuses. The pastor spoke of Fry's penis "terrorizing someone," at which point Stephen Fry, part outraged and part bemused, said he just wasn't interested in sodomy or buggery. This seemed to confuse the pastor, who insisted on knowing when Fry first had homosexual intercourse. Fry replied, "I've never had it, never, most gays don't." The clearly confused man of God asked Fry if he had ever had a partner. Yes, said Fry, and had enjoyed other forms of sexual intimacy but not sodomy. The bewilderment on the lunatic's face is obvious. All of his bigoted, ignorant, and hysterical stereotypes and prejudices were suddenly exploded by a very clever, urbane, and gay Englishman. Fry, by the way, got married two years later and is very happy. I've no idea what the pastor is doing but gays in Uganda still face the most violent and degrading persecution.

The dehumanizing of gay people by those who claim to follow Christ takes on many forms. I personally heard a prominent Christian minister explain to a congregation of more than a thousand people how the rate of suicide among gay teens was much higher than among straight teenagers, thus proving that self-loathing, emotional instability, depression, and turmoil were somehow inherent in homosexuality. He was right that suicide and attempted suicide rates are appallingly high among gay teens but the exact reason for that, and their feelings of isolation and mental pain, is that people such as the minister say such disdainful things about them. Teenage years are challenging enough for straight people so imagine the difficulties facing gay teens. When I privately challenged the minister after the service, I was told that I was either naïve or had "bought into the agenda." The lack of genuine concern for gay victims and the use of such suffering to try to enforce a religious position is deeply disturbing.

The truth is that, as I wrote earlier, the secular arguments and their religious extensions do not stand up to scrutiny – most of them have been defeated and dismissed in law courts and in political debate. Because the secular argument is to a very large extent won, the faith argument remains alone in opposing equal marriage and that makes me more sorry than I can ever express. The standard mantra, as we have seen, is that opponents of marriage equality do not hate homosexuals but reject homosexuality and they do not hate the sinner but they do hate sin. I wonder how they would respond if gay people argued that they do not hate heterosexuals but do condemn heterosexuality and they do not hate the sinner but they do hate the sin? The Christian proposition insists that a loving relationship between consenting adults is sinful and then it assumes that sexuality – in its emotional, intellectual, spiritual, and sexual aspects – can be separated from the individual. That's too callow to be taken seriously. We can love an alcoholic but despise his alcoholism or love a drug addict but despise his habit, but a physical and mental addiction to a harmful substance that leads to decay, suffering, and premature death is not akin on any level to a person's love for another human being. As for this being about the Christian concern for those who are not saved, as a Jewish friend once said to me about the Christian attempt to convert Jews and its historic link to anti-Semitism, "I wish they'd stop loving us so much!"

Richard Coles is probably the only Anglican priest to have once been a pop star. He was part of The Communards, who gave us "Don't Leave Me This Way," the best-selling single of 1986 and a song to which I still dance – much to my joy and my family's embarrassment. Coles is a tremendous spokesman for Christianity, is openly gay, and is generally careful not to overly condemn his critics and to look for the positive in any situation. But even he says, "The Church should repent of its hostility to homosexual people and beg forgiveness for its treatment of the gay community. . . . You cannot be a Christian homophobe." He also says, touchingly and poignantly, of his sexuality, "I'd got out of the habit of self-loathing. In the love of Jesus Christ I discovered I was not so loathsome nor so special as I thought I was." [6] All of us, straight and gay, have to establish a new Christian approach that emphasizes inclusion over exclusion. Nobody is loathsome to Christ, even the homophobe. But Coles is correct in that the first step for organized Christianity must be contrition. Saying sorry is never easy but it's always very Christian. I quoted Dr. Jeffrey John, the dean of St. Albans, earlier and he remains a lyrical, gentle, and just voice for the cause of equal marriage. Thus I proudly quote him again. In a video he made for the Out4Marriage campaign in 2012, he spoke of his frustration at the way he and other gay Christians have been treated: "I am sad because the Church that I love and serve is opposing it, when it should be rejoicing at it and sad because the Church is meant to show Christ's face to the world and on this subject, it doesn't." He continued, "If you are gay, please don't judge God by the Church. The official Church doesn't speak with integrity on this issue and so, frankly, doesn't deserve to be listened to. If you are gay, then please understand that God made you as you are, and loves you as you are, and if you invite him into your relationship, then of course he will bless you and sustain your love just as much as he blesses and sustains any other marriage. I know that's true from my own experience and that's why I'm 'out for marriage', because I'm sure God is too."

Reverend Dr. Giles Fraser also put it very well in a broadcast on BBC Radio 4 as part of the corporation's "Thought for the Day" series. Fraser is an Anglican priest, a journalist, and an activist. He is not gay. "If anything, it's more difficult with religion where this attitude towards homosexuality can commonly be presented as having some moral or theological justification. But despite the widespread perception that faith is uniformly hostile to homosexuality, there are a significant number of people of faith who want to offer a minority report that insists being gay is no sort of moral issue – indeed, that the ways in which two adults express their love for each other physically ought to be celebrated as something precious, as something publicly to affirm. What makes homophobia so especially wicked is that it traps people into a miserable life of clandestine relationships, continually fearful that they might one day be discovered and exposed for who they really are. Which is why having the guts to make such a public declaration of being gay, thus risking insults and name-calling – and in some countries considerably worse – is such a powerful witness to the truth."

Let me conclude with a personal story. I graduated from high school in England in 1977. There was a somewhat perfunctory party at which students and teachers said goodbye to one another, but most of us were only too eager to see the back of school and go on to university, work, fun, whatever. I remained close to my oldest friend, who later was best man at my wedding, but otherwise I have not maintained contact with most of my contemporaries. Frankly, I can't even remember many of their names.

There was one couple, however, that I do remember: Jonathan and Angela. I say "couple" because while only seventeen years old back then they always seemed to have been together. Not in some prurient way but as surprisingly mature, committed young people. They were also both extremely good-looking, athletic, and intelligent. With so many gifts, they could at least have been unpleasant and rude just to balance things out but they were kind and generous too. The model couple.

I recall Angela speaking to me at the party about her plans, but I think I was too busy trying to look at her legs to listen to what she was saying. After that I pretty much forgot about Angela and Jonathan. I married, came to Canada, started a family, moved on.

Fast-forward twenty years and a phone call from that oldest friend. "Are you still visiting London at Christmas, and do you remember Jonathan and Angela?" he asked. I said yes to both questions. "They've apparently been living in Africa and have just returned to Britain. They're having a party to say hello to everybody. They want us all to know, however, that Jonathan was in an accident. Angela had been a teacher at a small school, and there had been a fire. One little boy, Joshua, had been left inside. Jonathan ran back in and rescued the boy. The child is fine, but Jonathan is badly burnt – they don't want anybody to be shocked when they see him."

I did indeed fly to London that Christmas and made my way to the apartment where Jonathan and Angela were staying. It was Christmas Eve, and I'd planned to go to Midnight Mass after seeing them. As for burns and the accident, I had worked as a war reporter, had seen death up close, and was – I foolishly prided myself – a man of the world. I arrived a little early and knocked on the door. There was Angela, as lovely as ever. "Come in, come in," she said. "You're the first one here, and Jonathan will be overjoyed so see you."

There he was. This once strikingly handsome young man, sitting in a large armchair, his face so disguised by scar tissue that I could barely see his eyes. One ear seemed to be almost missing, and he had hardly any hair. I tried to register nonchalance, but it didn't work. Then he spoke, and the voice was the same as it had been two decades earlier. "All right, Coren, I know I look a bloody mess. But at least one of us has kept their figure."

I tried to laugh, but instead I began to cry. Angela ran to me, embraced me, said, "Don't worry, don't worry, we've both done a lot of that. Don't worry." Then a little African boy ran into the room, jumped on Jonathan's lap, and said, "Daddy, Daddy." Angela held my hand and said, "Have you met our new adopted son? His name is Joshua."

I learned that night that Jonathan and Angela were Christians and had been for most of their lives. After they left university, they had worked as missionaries in Africa, he helping to bring a clean water supply to the region and she setting up and running a school. Christ had formed their lives, their behaviour, their relationship, their love, their sacrifice, and their courage. I should have known this all those years earlier but I was too busy thinking of myself, my ambition, and what I wanted to do. Too busy trying to look at Angela's legs. That was an evening, a Christmas, and a Midnight Mass I will never forget.

Let me be candid. There are times when I wonder if it's all worth it. The internal politics of the Christian church, the ambitious Christians who gossip and betray and those who say they follow Jesus but are never happy unless they are condemning and criticizing other people's words and actions. But whenever I feel the sting, see the unfairness, or shudder at the injustice, I try to think of Jonathan, Angela, and little Joshua. But most of all I think of what the faith is all about, and it is about Jesus Christ, who loves all and does not judge. I tell this story here because I believe that the welcoming of gay people, who have suffered at Christian hands for so long, is at the epicentre of the modern Christian challenge and that by washing away the stains of prejudice and discrimination we can spark a new awakening. I have not had to run into any burning schools or put my life at risk and my complaints in the first chapter of the book about ill treatment are generally little more than privileged whines compared to what so many gay Christians have been treated to. God forgive us. He became a baby so that we could know Him and understand Him properly. This is the Christ story, the story of God becoming man becoming child. Naked vulnerability guaranteeing eternal life. Angela reminded me of this when I spoke to her the day before I returned to Canada those nearly-twenty years ago. "Women used to turn and look at my husband in the street because he was so good-looking," she said. "Now everybody turns and looks at him, but for other reasons." A pause. "I've never stopped looking at him, and never will."

Never stop looking at Jesus, as a baby, a child, an adult, a man dying on a cross, a God restored to life, a saviour with us until the end of time. Never stop looking at the world as a place of love and never stop embracing and accepting that love. If two men or two women commit to one another in a devoted, sacrificial, committed, and faithful marriage, the Christ-centred world of love is made deeper, wider, and better. As Christ Himself says in the first words he utters in the Gospel of Mark, we must open our hearts and believe the Good News. The Greek word used here is actually *metanoeite*, literally *to change your minds* but is usually translated as *repent* or *convert*. I prefer the more accurate translation and know that a transformation to what is true and good is a gift to God. Being open to change. Yes, that's it. That is my epiphany, that is my heart and mind changed, a Christian's heart and mind changed. Pray God we can all accept that splendid reality and that this debate will finally be over because it is quite simply unnecessary. God be praised.

# NOTES

## SO THIS IS HOW IT FEELS

1. In response to my article in the *New York Daily News*, September 22, 2013.
2. *Theatre Royal: 100 Years of Stratford East* (1984, Quartet).
3. "I Was Wrong," Sun Newspaper Chain, June 28, 2014.
4. "Michael Coren Complicit in Destruction of Souls Who Practice Homosexuality, Pt 1," http://signofcontradiction.blogspot. ca/2014/02/michael-coren-complicit-in-destruction.html, Contra/ Diction! February 13, 2014.
5. Mark Oakley, *The Collage of God* (2001, Darton, Longman & Todd).

## BIBLE BELIEVING

1. Malcolm Johnson, *Diary of a Gay Priest: The Tightrope Walker* (2013, Christian Alternative).
2. The letter seemed to first appear in 2000, and while some people have claimed authorship, the origin is not completely certain.
3. Emo Phillips, "The Best God Joke Ever – and It's Mine!" *The Guardian*, September 29, 2005. (http://www.theguardian.com/ stage/2005/sep/29/comedy.religion)
4. Alan Wilson, "Any 'Biblical' Objection to Gay Marriage Is Nonsense. The C of E Must Admit This." *The Guardian*, October 6, 2014. (http://www.theguardian.com/commentisfree/2014/oct/06 /biblical-objection-gay-marriage-church-of-england)
5. Jeffrey John, *Permanent, Faithful, Stable* (1993, Darton, Longman & Todd Ltd.).
6. Tobin Grant, "Opposition to Interracial Marriage Lingers Among Evangelicals." *Gleanings Magazine*, June 24, 2011.

(http://www.christianitytoday.com/gleanings/2011/june/opposition
-to-interracial-marriage-lingers-among.html)

7. K.J. Dover, *Greek Homosexuality* (1978, Harvard University Press);
   Bernard Sergent, *Homosexuality in Greek Myth* (1986, Beacon Press).

8. Richard L Hasbany, *Homosexuality and Religion* (1990, Harrington
   Park Press).

9. Charles Humana, *The Keeper of the Bed: The Story of the Eunuch*
   (1973, Arlington Books).

10. Dr. Nancy Wilson, *Outing the Church* (2013, LifeJourney Press).

11. In Kings, widows approach Elijah and Elisha for support, and
    in Genesis we see Judah telling his daughter-in-law, Tamar,
    that she has to return to her father's house when she becomes
    a widow.

12. John R. Coats, "Were Sodom and Gomorrah Really Torched for
    Homosexuality?" *Huff Post Religion*, huffingtonpost.com, July 26,
    2010. (http://www.huffingtonpost.com/john-r-coats/were-sodom
    -and-gomorrah-r_b_656178.html)

13. John Boswell, *Christianity, Social Tolerance, and Homosexuality*
    (1980, University of Chicago).

14. James V. Brownson, *Bible, Gender, Sexuality: Reframing the Church's
    Debate on Same-Sex Relationships* (2013, Eerdmans).

15. For example, in the *Sibylline Oracles*, a collection of utterances
    from the second to sixth centuries.

16. Daniel Helminiak, *What the Bible Really Says About Homosexuality*
    (1994, Alamo Square Press).

17. Ibid.

## ON THE FRONT LINE

1. All these interviews were recorded personally by the author in
   2014 and 2015.

2. Published by Green Bridge, 2012.

## THE FUTURE

1. Stephen Bates, *A Church at War* (2004, Taurus).

2. Gene Robinson, *God Believes in Love: Straight Talk About Gay
   Marriage* (2013, Vintage).

3. Extensive comments at http://www.scottlively.net.

4. Personal letter to the author.

5. Tony Campolo's personal website, June 8, 2015. http://tonycampolo .org/for-the-record-tony-campolo-releases-a-new-statement/# .VeNLL7xViko.

6. Patrick Strudwick, "Vicky Beeching, Christian Rock Star: I'm Gay. God Loves Me Just the Way I Am." *The Independent*, August 13, 2014. (http://www.independent.co.uk/news/people/news/vicky-beeching-star-of-the-christian-rock-scene-im-gay-god-loves-me-just-the-way-i-am-9667566.html)

7. Steve Chalke, "A Matter of Integrity: The Church, Sexuality, Inclusion and an Open Conversation." *Christianity*, January 2013.

8. *The Sean Hannity Show*, June 26, 2015, Fox News.

9. Franklin Graham, "Putin's Olympic Controversy." *Decision Magazine*, February 28, 2014. (http://billygraham.org/decision-magazine/march-2014/putins-olympic-controversy/)

10. Kyle Roberts, "Gay Christian Employee Leaves Wheaton College." Patheos: Hosting the Conversation on Faith, July 14, 2015. http://www.patheos.com/blogs/unsystematictheology /2015/07/gay-christian-employee-leaves-wheaton-college.

11. Rachel Donadio, "On Gay Priests, Pope Francis Asks, 'Who Am I to Judge?'" *New York Times*, July 29, 2013. (http://www.nytimes.com /2013/07/30/world/europe/pope-francis-gay-priests.html?_r=0)

12. Joshua J. McElwee, "Francis Strongly Criticizes Gender Theory, Comparing It to Nuclear Arms." *National Catholic Reporter*, February 13, 2015. (http://ncronline.org/news/vatican/francis -strongly-criticizes-gender-theory-comparing-nuclear-arms)

13. Edward Pentin, "Cardinal Bergoglio Hits Out at Same-Sex Marriage." *National Catholic Register*, July 8, 2010. (http://www.ncregister.com/blog /edward-pentin/cardinal_bergoglio_hits_out_at_same-sex_marriage #view-comments)

14. *Catechism of the Catholic Church*.

15. 2006 speech in Los Angeles and *The Tablet* 2005.

16. Carol Kuruvilla, "Belgian Catholic Bishop Calls for Recognition of Same-Sex Relationships." *Huffington Post*, December 31, 2014.

(http://www.huffingtonpost.com/2014/12/31/belgian-bishop-gay
-marriage-_n_6401560.html)

17. https://www.lifesitenews.com/opinion/pope-francis-and
-homosexuality-confusing-signs Die Tagespost, June 8, 2015.
18. CBS News, "Archbishop: School That Fired Gay Teacher Showed
'Common Sense.'" July 13, 2015. (http://www.cbsnews.com/news
/philly-archbishop-school-that-fired-gay-teacher-showed
-common-sense/)
19. Diarmaid MacCulloch, "A Different Cloth," review of *Newman's
Unquiet Grave: The Reluctant Saint* by John Cornwell, *Literary Review*,
June 2010.

## LAST WORDS

1. Stephanie Pappas, "Why Gay Parents May Be the Best Parents."
*LiveScience*, January 15, 2012. (http://www.livescience.com/17913
-advantages-gay-parents.html)
2. Jesse Singal, "How Scientists Debunked the Biggest Anti-Gay-
Marriage Study." *New York Magazine*, May 19, 2015. (http://nymag.com
/scienceofus/2015/05/biggest-anti-gay-marriage-study-was-debunked
.html)
3. John Corvino, *What's Wrong with Homosexuality?* (2013, Oxford).
4. Ryan Lenz, "NARTH Becomes Main Source for Anti-Gay 'Junk
Science.'" Southern Poverty Law Center, March 1, 2012. (https://
www.splcenter.org/fighting-hate/intelligence-report
/2012/narth-becomes-main-source-anti-gay-'junk-science')
5. Amanda Hess, "Mythbusting: What Gay Men Really Do in Bed."
*GOOD*, October 2011. (http://magazine.good.is/articles
/gay-sex-is-not-anal-sex)
6. Patrick Strudwick, "Richard Coles: My Journey From Pop Star to
Celibate Vicar." *The Independent*, October 13, 2014. (http://www.
independent.co.uk/news/people/richard-coles
-my-journey-from-pop-star-to-celibate-vicar-9792279.html)

# BIBLIOGRAPHY

There are a number of works written about the subjects covered in this book and this is merely a list of those that have been particularly helpful to me.

Adams, Elizabeth. *Going to Heaven*. Soft Skull, 2006.

Alexander, J. Neil. *This Far by Grace*. Cowley, 2003.

Bates, Stephen. *A Church at War*. IB Tauris, 2004.

Boswell, John. *Same-Sex Unions in Premodern Europe*. Villard, 1994.

Coles, Richard. *Fathomless Riches*. Weidenfeld & Nicolson, 2014.

Corvino, John. *What's Wrong with Homosexuality*. Oxford, 2013.

Helminiak, Daniel A. *What the Bible Really Says about Homosexuality*. Alamo Square, 1994.

John, Jeffrey. *Permanent, Faithful, Stable*. DLT, 1993.

Johnson, Malcolm. *Diary of a Gay Priest: The Tightrope Walker*. Christian Alternative, 2013.

MacCulloch, Diarmaid. *Christianity: The First Three Thousand Years*. Penguin, 2009.

Oakley, Mark. *The Collage of God*. DLT, 2001.

Stock, Victor. *Taking Stock*. Harper Collins, 2001.

Sullivan, Andrew. *Virtually Normal*. Knopf, 1995.

Vines, Matthew. *God and the Gay Christian*. Convergent, 2014.

Wilson, Alan. *More Perfect Union?* DLT, 2014.

author photo courtesy of SUN News Network

MICHAEL COREN is the bestselling author of sixteen books, including biographies of G.K. Chesterton, H.G. Wells, Arthur Conan Doyle, J.R.R. Tolkien, and C.S. Lewis. He is the host of the talk show "The Arena" on the SUN News Network. He also writes a syndicated column for ten daily newspapers, and was recently named the columnist of the year by the Catholic Press Association. His book *Why Catholics Are Right* was a national bestseller.

## A NOTE ABOUT THE TYPE

*Epiphany* is set in Monotype Dante, a modern font family designed by Giovanni Mardersteig in the late 1940s. Based on the classic book faces of Bembo and Centaur, Dante features an italic, which harmonizes extremely well with its roman partner. The digital version of Dante was issued in 1993, in three weights and including a set of titling capitals.